Upper Primary

Natural disasters

NATURE IN TURMOIL

Published by Prim-Ed Publishing

www.prim-ed.com

6424C

LITERACY AND GEOGRAPHY THEME
Natural disasters

Published by Prim-Ed Publishing® 2006
Reprinted under licence by Prim-Ed Publishing 2006
Copyright© R.I.C. Publications® 2005
ISBN 1 84654 069 0
PR–6424

Additional titles available in this series:
Antarctica
Rainforests
Environmental issues

This master may only be reproduced by the original purchaser for use with their class(es). The publisher prohibits the loaning or onselling of this master for the purposes of reproduction.

Copyright Notice

Blackline masters or copy masters are published and sold with a limited copyright. This copyright allows publishers to provide teachers and schools with a wide range of learning activities without copyright being breached. This limited copyright allows the purchaser to make sufficient copies for use within their own education institution. The copyright is not transferable, nor can it be onsold. Following these instructions is not essential but will ensure that you, as the purchaser, have evidence of legal ownership to the copyright if inspection occurs.

For your added protection in the case of copyright inspection, please complete the form below. Retain this form, the complete original document and the invoice or receipt as proof of purchase.

Name of Purchaser:

_____

Date of Purchase:

_____

Supplier:

_____

School Order# (if applicable):

_____

Signature of Purchaser:

_____

Internet websites

In some cases, websites or specific URLs may be recommended. While these are checked and rechecked at the time of publication, the publisher has no control over any subsequent changes which may be made to webpages. It is *strongly* recommended that the class teacher checks *all* URLs before allowing pupils to access them.

View all pages online

Website: www.prim-ed.com

Email: sales@prim-ed.com

Foreword

Natural disasters is one of a series of four books designed specifically for upper primary pupils.

A natural disaster is a major catastrophe caused by nature. Usually widespread destruction, both materially and in lost lives or injury, accompany a natural disaster.

The ten natural disasters included in this book include tsunamis; volcanic eruptions; earthquakes; cyclones, hurricanes and typhoons; plagues, epidemics and pandemics; avalanches, mudslides and landslides; drought; storms and floods; tornadoes and bushfires.

The wide variety of activities in this book cross all major learning areas.

Titles in this series include:
- *Natural disasters*
- *Rainforests*
- *Antarctica*
- *Environmental issues*

Contents

Teachers notes .... iv – v
Natural disasters overview .... vi – ix
Natural disasters time line .... x – xi
Emergency procedures and
preventative measures .... xii – xvii
Quiz questions .... xviii – xxv
Quiz answers xxvi
Curriculum links xxvii

Tsunamis 2–9
Tsunamis 2–4
Tsunami poster 5
Ring of Fire 6–8
Ring of Fire mapping 9

Volcanic eruptions 10–17
Volcanic eruptions 10–12
Make a volcano 13
Volcanic disasters 14–16
Volcanic legends 17

Earthquakes 18–25
Earthquakes 18–20
Earthquake crossword 21
The effects of earthquakes 22–24
Newspaper report 25

Cyclones, hurricanes and typhoons 26–33
Cyclones, hurricanes and typhoons 26–28
Cyclonic crossword 29
Cyclone Tracy 30–32
Cyclone shelter design 33

Plagues, epidemics and pandemics 34–41
Plagues, epidemics and pandemics 34–36
Plague of words 37
The bubonic plague 38–40
Plague poetry 41

Avalanches, landslides and mudslides 42–49
Avalanches, landslides and mudslides 42–44
Alaskan avalanche poem 45
Thredbo Ski Resort landslide 46–48
Grim gadgets 49

Drought 50–53
Drought 50–52
Concert creation 53

Storms and floods 54–57
Storms and floods 54–56
The storm spotter! 57

Tornadoes 58–61
Tornadoes 58–60
Tornado experiments 61

Bushfires 62–65
Bushfires 62–64
Bushfire vocabulary 65

Prim-Ed Publishing   www.prim-ed.com

Natural disasters

Teachers notes

The ten natural disasters covered in this book follow a similar format.

Each natural disaster is divided into a unit of one or two groups of four pages:

- a teachers page
- a pupil information page
- a pupil comprehension page
- a cross-curricular activity.

An **overview** for teachers has been included on pages vi – ix with suggestions for activities to further develop the theme with the whole class or as extension work for more able pupils.

A **time line** of natural disasters has been provided on pages x – xi. These include a selection over the past 3500 years.

Emergency procedures and preventative measures for the natural disasters covered are provided on pages xii – xvii. These are an easily accessible accompaniment to each disaster, being able to be photocopied and separated for discussion, display or as a ready reference.

NOTE: While every endeavour has been taken by the authors to include correct emergency procedures, more specific information may be obtained by contacting the emergency organisations.

Teachers page

The teachers page has the following information:

Objectives state literacy objectives for reading and comprehending the informational text and objectives relating to the cross-curricular pupil page.

Page numbers for **quiz questions** relating to the section are given in the worksheet information section.

Answers are given for all questions, where applicable. Open-ended tasks require the teacher to check the answers.

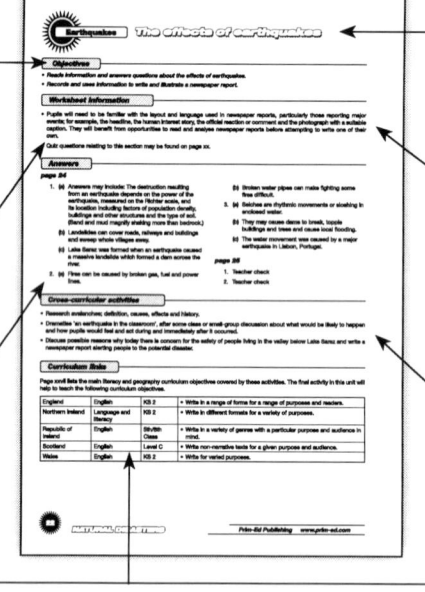

The **title of the text** indicates the natural disaster or one example of that particular natural disaster.

Worksheet information details any background information required by the teacher about the disaster, or presents specific details regarding the use of the worksheets.

Cross-curricular activities suggest further activities to develop the topic in the same, or another, learning area.

Curriculum links are given for:
- the geography-based theme (page xxvii)
- the literacy-based comprehension activity (page xxvii)
- the cross-curricular activity.

Quiz questions

Quiz questions with answers are given for each section on pages xviii to xxvi.

The quiz questions are presented in a 'half-page' card format for ease of photocopying and may be:

- given orally, with pupils answering on a separate sheet of paper,
- photocopied and given individually as a written test,
- combined with the other appropriate pages from the unit(s) as a final assessment of the topic, or
- photocopied and used by pairs or groups of pupils as 'quick quiz' activities.

Prim-Ed Publishing   www.prim-ed.com

Teachers notes

Natural disasters

The pupil pages follow the format below.

- The first pupil page is an informational text, usually providing general information about how each disaster occurs, what happens during the disaster, a diagram (if relevant), the aftermath of the disaster and some history about the particular type of disaster, with examples.

- The second pupil page is a comprehension page to gauge pupil understanding of the text. A variety of activities are provided, including answering literal, deductive and evaluative questions, compiling information for a retrieval chart, completing diagrams or maps, and cloze activities.

- The final pupil page is a cross-curricular activity. Occasionally, these activities may all fall within the same learning area such as English.

Pupil pages

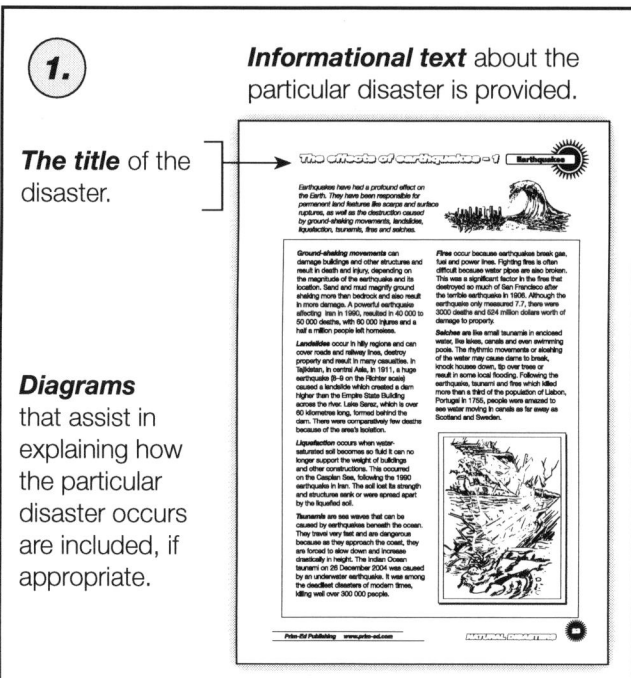

1.

The title of the disaster.

Informational text about the particular disaster is provided.

Diagrams that assist in explaining how the particular disaster occurs are included, if appropriate.

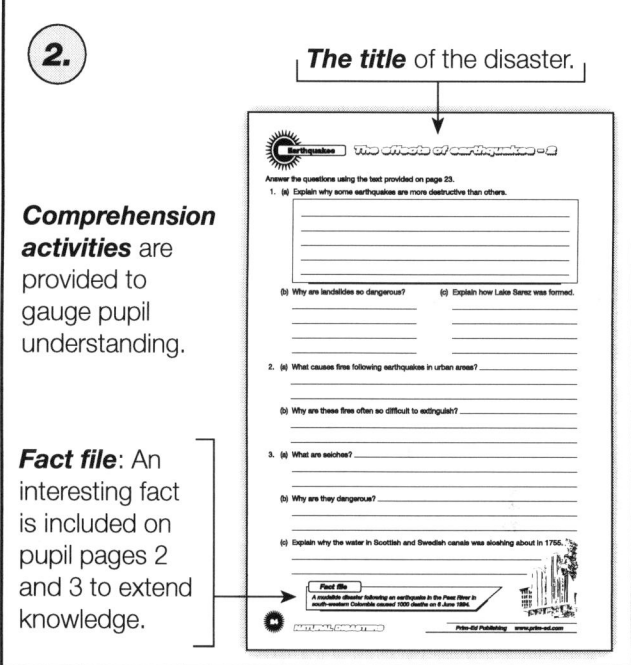

2.

The title of the disaster.

Comprehension activities are provided to gauge pupil understanding.

Fact file: An interesting fact is included on pupil pages 2 and 3 to extend knowledge.

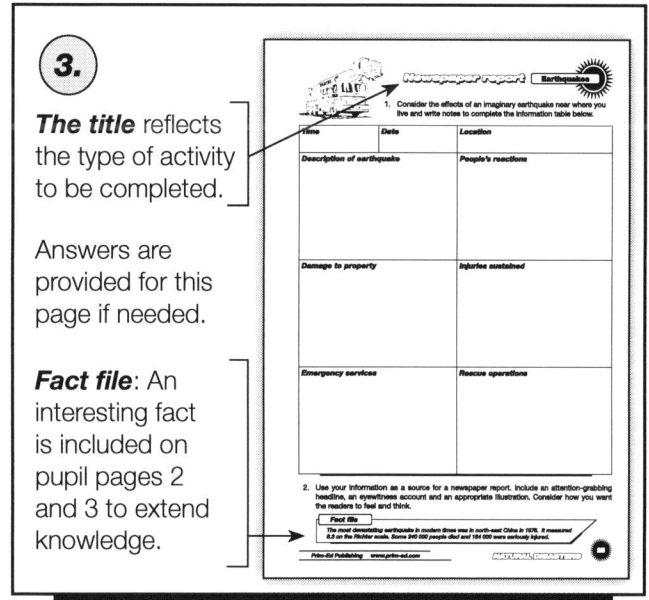

3.

The title reflects the type of activity to be completed.

Answers are provided for this page if needed.

Fact file: An interesting fact is included on pupil pages 2 and 3 to extend knowledge.

Prim-Ed Publishing   www.prim-ed.com

NATURAL DISASTERS

 **Natural disasters**

The cross-curricular activities suggested below may aid in developing the theme.

English

- Ask pupils to research and write reports about selected natural disasters which have occurred over the last fifteen years. Collate these into a class book.
- Write a series of 'Which disaster am I?' questions for pupils to answer.
- Use several resources, including websites, to research the occurrence of a natural disaster. Make notes from each resource and use them to write a report on the disaster. Write the report for either television or a newspaper.
- Choose a natural disaster and write a descriptive report, with illustrations, about how it is generated. Your audience will be younger pupils.
- Write a narrative poem about a natural disaster.
- Interview a disaster survivor for a personal account of his/her experiences.
- Write an acrostic poem using the letters in the name of a specific natural disaster; e.g. TSUNAMI, CYCLONE, BLACK DEATH.
- Write an emotive recount of a natural disaster from an 'eyewitness' point of view.
- Listen to a weather expert or scientist speak about the dangers of different natural disasters.
- Write poems using words that describe feelings people might have when experiencing a natural disaster.
- Write a list of qualities you think natural disaster experts like vulcanologists should have.
- Write a narrative story about a group of children caught in a basement during a flash flood. How do they escape? Are they heroes? Who else do they save?
- View photographs of spectacular storms and write about them.
- Write a poem that helps to raise awareness of the everyday suffering in Africa as a result of starvation.

Maths

- Tally and graph the number of lives lost and the cost of specific natural disasters.
- Draw up a table showing the seven continents and three chosen natural disasters. Research to discover how many of each disaster has occurred in each continent in the last ten years. Complete the table and present the data in graphical form. Record any conclusions that may be drawn from the graph.
- Select three occurrences of a specific natural disaster. Tabulate and compare all the data provided, reporting on similarities and differences.
- Write five mathematical facts about one particular natural disaster.
- Compare two disasters and calculate the differences between when they occurred, the number of fatalities, the numbers injured and the estimated costs.
- Calculate how much water your family would need for three days following a disaster.
- Rank a series of disasters according to the severity: number of deaths, number injured, number homeless, amount of money to repair damage etc.
- Discover how earthquakes are measured, how the velocity of wind in a cyclone is measured and how it is ranked in severity etc.
- Compile a list of mathematical facts about a series of natural disasters.
- Discover how the intensity of a volcano can be measured.
- Find out the way to measure how far away a storm is. (Hint: It involves lightning and thunder!)
- Find out how a severe thunderstorm is measured in your country.

Overview

Natural disasters

The cross-curricular activities suggested below may aid in developing the theme.

Geography and history

- Research changes to a community or the environment as the result of a natural disaster.

- Investigate how the basic needs of survivors of a natural disaster are met.

- Study a portion of a map of the ocean floor. Note the names of the plates, trenches, mountain ranges and any other features. Research how these features are linked to natural disasters.

- Study an area of the planet where a particular natural disaster is prevalent. Research the physical geography of the area and give reasons for the occurrence of this phenomenon. Write a time line indicating the most recent events.

- List the basic needs of survivors after a disaster, in order of importance.

- List the different types of transport used in your community, the ways in which each could be disrupted by a natural disaster and what effect this could have.

- Read disaster scenarios and decide on the appropriate action to take for each one.

- Invite a volunteer emergency services member to speak to the class about their job. Pupils compile a list of questions to ask.

- On a map of the world, mark where different types of natural disaster are likely to occur.

- Research to find out about storms and floods in the local area. What safety measures are in place? Create an information poster about the local area and the risk of danger from storms and/or floods. Give the town a risk rating out of 10.

- Africa is a continent that suffers greatly from drought. Research other countries/continents that experience drought. Use a world map to mark these countries. Create a colour-coded key that shows the severity of the drought experienced.

- Construct a time line and plot well-known natural disasters on it.

Science

- Describe, using models or displays, how a natural disaster occurs.

- Evaluate built environments for their ability to withstand specific natural disasters.

- Research the names and methods of use of instruments which are employed in the detection and measurement of natural disasters. Draw a diagram of each, explaining simply its use and what the measurements mean.

- Research how architects and builders are designing buildings to withstand the force of natural disasters.

- Research the different forms of communication used in your locality. How would each function following a natural disaster?

- Many people are electrocuted in the aftermath of a disaster. Explain why this happens.

- Read accounts of animals' behaviour preceding a natural disaster.

- Research the effects 'El Niño' and 'La Niña' have on the occurrence of natural disasters.

- Discuss some of the scientific principles behind the phenomena that lead to or cause natural disasters.

- Investigate the effects specified types of natural disasters have on the environment.

- Make 'lightning' by using a baking tray, modelling clay, a large plastic bag and a metal lid from a jar (or a coin). Place the tray on the plastic bag. Attach the dough to the tray. Move the tray around using the ball of dough as a handle. Pick up the tray only and place the metal lid close to it. What happens?

- Use objects such as fur, woollen cloth, balloons, plastic pens and rulers etc. to observe the effects of static electricity.

- Create the effect of a dust storm and wind erosion using a hairdryer and flat tray filled with dirt, rocks, sand and twigs. Remove the twigs and rocks and try again. Notice the increase in erosion when the soil is void of vegetation or heavier material to help 'hold it together'.

Prim-Ed Publishing   www.prim-ed.com

 **Natural disasters**

The cross-curricular activities suggested below may aid in developing the theme.

The arts

(Music, drama, visual arts)

- Add sound effects or a simple tune to a poem about a specific natural disaster.

- Create an artwork about a natural disaster using dramatic colours or materials. One example may be to create a scene using red and orange crayons or other medium that shows the dry, cracked earth of a drought-stricken land.

- Use different materials to decorate a large outline or flow diagram of the generation of a natural disaster.

- Using a range of percussion instruments with varying tone and timbre, compose a musical piece to illustrate the generation of a natural disaster.

- Dramatise the reactions of specific groups of people to a natural disaster.

- Illustrate a sequence of events in a natural disaster using a cartoon format and speech balloons.

- Prepare a chart or poster to inform people what to do in a particular disaster. Include illustrations.

- Listen to and compare film soundtracks accompanying disaster scenes.

- View photographs of different volcanic eruptions. Use the colours to inspire a range of paintings or drawings.

- Read a range of myths and legends that attempt to explain natural disasters. Use these to write and perform plays in small groups.

- Create a storm collage using pictures from magazines and other sources. Use other mediums to show the fierceness of your storm, such as aluminium foil for lightning, cotton wool painted black for a cloud etc.

- Represent 'St Elmo's Fire' as a piece of artwork. You may need to research it first!

- As a group, brainstorm ways to conserve water. Present the information as a poster that can be displayed in a well-used area of the school. Make the poster eye-catching and colourful.

Health and personal/social development

- Investigate and record the telephone numbers for emergency services in the local area.

- Develop a physical fitness programme to enable pupils to cope in times of stress such as a disaster. Include relaxation techniques.

- List the main problems people face when the infrastructure of their community is destroyed by a natural disaster.

- Investigate what can be done to relieve the situation of others following a natural disaster.

- Research worldwide disaster relief organisations.

- List the personal qualities needed by people who work in disaster relief.

- Read and discuss real-life stories of people who have survived natural disasters.

- Research how the lack of good hygiene practices and lack of plumbing in the past were largely responsible for waterborne diseases such as cholera being rampant. Relate to third world countries and outbreaks after natural disasters.

- Research to find out about the health problems that natural disasters can cause; e.g. disease, water pollution.

- Role-play different emergency responses for a range of natural disasters.

- Research how water is contaminated during a flood and how this affects people's health. Present your information as a five-minute speech to the class or a small group.

- Consider how the health of people can be affected by contaminated drinking water and research methods that can be used to purify water.

Overview

Natural disasters

The cross-curricular activities suggested below may aid in developing the theme.

DT and ICT

- Design a machine which detects natural disasters before they occur.

- Compile a natural disaster survival kit.

- Design a simple house. Create a natural force (e.g. fan heater, hairdryer). Build the house and determine how long it takes to collapse. Change the material or construction and repeat. Continue until the house withstands the force. Consider the properties required for strong construction.

- Design a tsunami simulator which shows the displacement of water and the tsunami train. (A tsunami 'train' is a series of successive tsunami waves.)

- List construction requirements for buildings in particular risk areas; e.g. floods, earthquakes, cyclones.

- Water contamination is often a problem after a natural disaster. Plan how a family could overcome this difficulty.

- Research the technology used to sterilise equipment to prevent contamination and the personal hygiene procedures surgeons follow. Compare with the past.

- Research to find out about early warning systems for different natural disasters.

- Design a travel brochure for a part of the world where a certain type of natural disaster is likely to occur. How do you warn potential tourists of possible dangers without scaring them away?

- Research houses that are built to withstand earthquakes. How are they different from other houses?

- Design a dam that has an in-built mechanism that prevents it from bursting. Make a model using modelling clay, wooden sticks, cellophane and other household items. Present your model to the class and explain the mechanism.

- Use the Internet to find a 'meteorology' website for your area; for example, www.metoffice.gov.uk

  Write a review of the website considering criteria such as:
  - Is it user-friendly?
  - Is it aesthetically pleasing?
  - Does it include colour photographs?
  - Does it include safety warnings for floods, storms etc?

- Design and make a rain gauge using household materials. Make your gauge environmentally friendly and aesthetically pleasing.

- Design a machine that could be placed in a paddock that would collect water and allow sheep to drink from it. It will need to be watertight. You may need to consider how to filter out any debris or unwanted objects.

Prim-Ed Publishing   www.prim-ed.com

 **Natural disasters**  **Time line**

The disasters listed in the time line below are a selection only and by no means exhaustive.

1650 BC
At Santorini Island in the Mediterranean Sea, an eruption kills thousands of people. Estimates of the number of people who died vary, but this eruption is significant as it is thought to be the source of the legend of Atlantis.

218 BC
Hannibal, a Carthaginian general, crosses the Italian Alps to conquer Rome; 18 000 soldiers, 2000 horses and many elephants die, mostly due to avalanches.

1330s–1340s
The 'black death' or bubonic plague strikes Europe and Asia. Spread by infected fleas and rats, it kills 75 million people.

1362
The Great Drowning in Holland kills some 30 000 people when the dykes holding back floodwaters break.

1556
In Huaxian, China, more than 830 000 people die as a result of a huge earthquake.

1737
Between 300 000 and 350 000 people drown and 20 000 vessels disappear when a cyclone hits the Hooghly River district of Bengal, India on October 7. This is considered the single worst cyclone disaster in history.

1755
Two massive earthquake shockwaves hit Lisbon, Portugal, destroying all buildings. Within half an hour, a huge tsunami train adds to the destruction. A fire which rages for three days, completes the devastation of what was the centre of the vast Portuguese empire; more than 90 000 people die.

1780
A hurricane in the Barbados area causes an estimated 22 000 deaths.

1815
The eruption of Mount Tambora in Sumbawa, Indonesia, is the most powerful in modern times. Over 90 000 people lose their lives in the earthquake and resulting tsunami. A major cause of death is starvation. The year following this double disaster is known as the year without a summer. Scientists have since found a connection between major volcanic eruptions and global cooling.

1825
In October, a large wildfire burns from Maine through to New Brunswick in Canada. Three million acres of forest are burned and more than 160 people die.

1863–1865
A London epidemic of smallpox kills 20 000 and disfigures survivors. The disease leaves deep pockmarks on the skin.

1876–1879
A deadly drought and famine hits China, killing over 9 000 000 people.

1883
An eruption at Krakatau, Indonesia, is estimated to have killed over 36 000 people, with a tsunami being the major cause of death. The explosion is thought to be the loudest sound ever heard on earth.

1887
The Yellow River (Huang He) floods in China, killing 900 000 people.

1896
An earthquake measuring 7.6 on the Richter scale and the massive tsunami generated by it, results in the death of 27 000 people in Honshu, Japan.

1900
The Indian drought brings about starvation and disease. It is believed that up to three and a quarter million people perish at the beginning of the century in India.

1902
Mt Pelee in Martinique erupts killing over 29 000 people – most of these due to ash flows. It is still an active volcano today.

1906
An earthquake causes 3000 deaths in the American city of San Francisco. Although only measuring 7.7 on the Richter Scale, the fires caused by broken fuel and power lines contributes to 524 million dollars worth of damage to property.

1907
Called the Chinese Famine, it is believed that 24 000 000 people die from starvation.

1910
118 people are trapped in a snowbound train in the Cascade Mountains in Wellington, Washington in the USA when an avalanche sweeps them into a gorge some 45 metres below the tracks.

1911
At Usoy, Tajikistan, an earthquake measuring 8–9 on the Richter Scale, triggers a landslide which forms a dam nearly 600 metres high on the Murgob River (higher than the Empire State Building in America!). A lake is created which is nearly 65 kilometres long. The death toll is not high because the area is sparsely populated.

1916
An epidemic of polio in the United States results in 27 000 people suffering paralysis and 6000 deaths.

1918–1919
A strain of influenza, most commonly known as the 'Spanish flu', kills between 20 and 40 million people.

1921–1922
Millions of people perish from drought in the Soviet Union.

1925
A 'Tri-state' tornado in the USA causes 695 deaths.

1933
An earthquake in Japan causes a tsunami which kills 3000 people on the island of Honshu and destroys 9000 homes.

1939–1945
Thirty million sheep are lost in Australia due to a prolonged drought.

1941–1942
Drought causes famine in China and 3 000 000 people perish.

1951
Some 250 people are killed and more than 45 000 trapped when a series of avalanches thunder through the Swiss, Austrian and Italian Alps.

1953
Believed to be one of Europe's worst natural disasters, a violent winter storm causes flooding and storm surges in the Netherlands and the United Kingdom. Over 2000 people perish.

Prim-Ed Publishing   www.prim-ed.com

Time line

Natural disasters

The disasters listed in the time line below are a selection only and by no means exhaustive.

1954
10 000 people suffer in Iran due to an extreme storm that produces flooding.

1962
About 4000 people are killed when tonnes of ice and snow slide down Huascaran Peak in the Andes Mountains in Peru.

1962–1965
A pandemic (German measles) affects approximately 12.5 million people in the United States alone, causing birth defects such as deafness and blindness to 20 000 infants.

1964
The strongest earthquake in the United States in the 20th century—8.6 on the Richter Scale—hits Anchorage, Alaska. Liquefaction of the soil caused by the vibrations results in huge landslides.

1965–1967
One and a half million people perish in India due to prolonged drought conditions.

1970
A cyclone-driven tsunami hits the Bay of Bengal, killing over 200 000 people. More than 100 000 people are unable to be found.

A landslide on the mountain slopes of Peru wipes out 10 villages and kills 20 000 people.

1971
Severe flooding in North Vietnam is caused by heavy rains; 1 000 000 people die.

1972
A four-year drought is broken in February in Iran. Unfortunately, a week of freezing snow causes approximately 4000 deaths.

1973
A monsoon in India kills 1200 people.

1974
Cyclone Tracy nearly destroys the city of Darwin in Australia, leading to a mass evacuation and leaving 65 dead.

1974
A 'Super tornado outbreak' in USA causes 315 deaths.

1980
A moderate earthquake causes rocks and mud to slide down a volcano at Mount St Helens in Washington State, USA. Pressure on the volcano is released and causes a major eruption on May 18. Although this is the largest landslide ever recorded, less than 60 people are killed because most had been evacuated. Thousands of deer and other animals, however, perish.

1980s–1990s
Outbreaks of mad cow disease—a fatal brain disorder—infect some 180 000 livestock in Europe and dozens of humans.

1981
On 21 November, 104 tornadoes hit Britain. This is the most tornadoes to hit any one country in Europe in one day.

1983
Ash Wednesday bushfire in South Australia and Victoria occurs; 3700 buildings are destroyed; 2400 homes lost; 76 people die; 1100 people are injured; 340 000 sheep and 18 000 cattle are lost; 20 000 kilometres of fences are destroyed. The total cost of the disaster is over $950 million.

1984–1985
Sahel in Africa, an area prone to drought, experiences a prolonged drought and famine with hundreds of thousands of lives lost.

1985
The Ruiz volcano in Colombia erupts with over 25 000 people killed, mainly due to mudflows.

1989
The deadliest tornado in history tears through Bangladesh, leaving 1300 people dead and 50 000 people homeless.

1990
A powerful earthquake (7.7 on the Richter Scale) in Iran during the night and in adverse weather conditions, results in between 40 000 and 50 000 deaths, 60 000 injuries and half a million people left homeless.

1991
A cyclone in SE Bangladesh kills 131 000 and leaves 9 000 000 homeless. Many survivors die from hunger or waterborne diseases.

1992
Hurricane Andrew hits the Bahamas, Florida and Louisiana and causes nearly $25 billion worth of damage, making it the second most expensive disaster in US history.

1995
El Niño causes great rains in California which bring about severe flooding.

1998
Thirty kilometres of the Papua New Guinea coastline are ravaged by a tsunami which follows two simultaneous earthquakes, each measuring 7 on the Richter scale. Many villages are totally destroyed and 5000 people lose their lives.

1999
In Turkey, an earth tremor measuring 7.6 on the Richter scale affects the north-west and central areas of the country. A devastating tsunami follows, resulting in a total death toll of 17 000.

A storm hits Sydney, Australia, with hail stones 13 cm in diameter and causes damage to 63 000 cars and 22 000 homes. One person is killed due to lightning.

2004
Over 300 000 people are killed by the tsunami which strikes south-east Asia after an earthquake in the Indian Ocean. Countries of East Africa, on the far side of the ocean are also affected. Indonesia in particular suffers great loss of life and injuries. Many communities are totally destroyed. Livelihood from employment such as tourism is greatly affected.

2005
On 29 August, Hurricane Katrina strikes New Orleans. Levees burst and flood the city; 1242 people die; $200 billion worth of damage is caused and over a million people are left homeless. Katrina is the most destructive and costliest natural disaster in US history.

On 5 October mudslides resulting from Hurricane Stan kill hundreds of people and leave half a million homeless in Central America and Mexico.

On 8 October, an earthquake measuring 7.6 strikes Pakistan and parts of India and Afghanistan, killing at least 18 000 people, injuring more than 40 000 and leaving at least 4 000 000 people homeless.

Emergency procedures

Tsunamis

Pages 2–9

Tsunamis can happen with very little warning. It is imperative that you move as far away from the coast as possible and as quickly as possible. When the first signs of a tsunami are apparent, there may be only minutes before the full force strikes.

You do not have much time!

- Learn about tsunamis. Know what the warning signs mean.
  A rapid rise or fall in water level means that the first tsunami wave is on its way. The second wave may be bigger and more forceful than the first.
- If you notice a rapid change in water level, move inland as far as possible or to the highest ground.
- If there is a drawback where the water recedes a long way, do not be tempted to investigate the debris left on the beach or catch any stranded fish.
  The next wave is on its way. Move quickly!
- If you are on a beach with warning sirens, take notice of them immediately. Move inland or to higher ground.
- Leave possessions behind.
- Move quickly but do not panic.

Volcanic eruptions

Pages 10–17

If you are near a volcano, always be on the watch for warning signs of eruptions. These include:
- rumbling noises, ash, gas and steam coming from the volcano
- earth tremors or earthquakes
- pumice dust in the air
- acid rain
- a 'rotten egg' smell

It is always better to evacuate an area before an eruption begins. If evacuation becomes necessary:

- Leave the area immediately, unless instructed by authorities to remain indoors. This may happen if you are some distance from the eruption but are in danger of ash fallout. Do not try to watch the eruption. Avoid areas downwind of the volcano and low-lying areas. Do not drive vehicles through ash fall.
- Wear safety gear to protect yourself from volcanic ash, gases, dust and flying debris. Cover your nose and mouth with a damp cloth or a dust mask, protect your eyes with safety goggles or glasses and wear thick clothing and a helmet or hat.
- Seek shelter in an underground emergency refuge. Only shelter in other buildings if you become trapped outdoors, as walls and roofs may collapse. If you become trapped indoors, close all windows and doors.

NATURAL DISASTERS — Prim-Ed Publishing   www.prim-ed.com

Emergency procedures

Earthquakes

Pages 18–25

During an earthquake:

- Stay calm.
- Stay indoors, away from windows.
- Turn off electrical appliances and gas.
- Crouch under a table, bench or in a doorway.
- If outside, stay away from trees, power poles and lines.
- If in a vehicle, stop, stay in vehicle away from buildings, trees, bridges and powerlines.

After an earthquake:

- Treat the injured.
- Put out fires and turn off gas.
- Don't use matches, candles or electrical appliances in case of gas leaks.
- Do not touch downed powerlines.
- Check water and food supply.
- Turn on battery-powered (or car) radios for information and instructions.
- Be prepared for aftershocks.

Cyclones, hurricanes and typhoons

Pages 26–33

As danger approaches:

- Check radio warnings often.
- Ensure the car is filled with fuel and move to a safe position.
- Be aware of safety routes.
- Check emergency supplies—tinned provisions, special medicines or drugs, batteries for torches or radios, fill bath with several days' supply of water, camp stove (with gas) and lights, sleeping bags.
- Turn refrigerator up as high as possible to make food last longer.
- Secure any loose property outside.
- Tape, board or shutter windows to prevent shattering; wedge sliding glass doors to prevent lifting from tracks.
- Move valuables as high as possible.

When the cyclone is nearly upon you:

- Stay clear of windows in the most sheltered part of your house on the downwind side.
- Stay indoors except in cases of extreme emergency.
- Bring in pets.
- Use the phone only for emergencies.

*If caught in an unprotected area, **stoop** or **crawl** to shelter.*

Prim-Ed Publishing   www.prim-ed.com

NATURAL DISASTERS

Emergency procedures

Avalanches, landslides and mudslides — Pages 42–49

If caught by an avalanche:

- Using 'swimming' motions, thrust upwards to try to stay close to the surface of the snow.
- Try to maintain an air pocket (to help you breathe) in front of your face, using hands and arms to 'punch' the snow.
- Breathe deeply to expand your chest; hold each breath to give a good space around you.
- Yell or make noise only when you hear rescuers near you; this helps to maintain your air supply.
- DO NOT PANIC – breathe steadily and remain calm.

If there is the possibility of a landslide or mudslide after a long period of rain:

- Remove debris from slopes.
- Before and during rain, frequently inspect the slope for downslope movements of materials, cracks, bulges at the base of slopes, holes or bare spots on slopes, tilting trees or streams becoming more muddied.
- Listen for rumbling sounds which may mean bedrock has shifted, breaking vegetation or structures.
- Monitor rain levels frequently using a gauge.
- Do not sleep in lower-floor bedrooms on the sides of houses which face slopes.

Drought — Pages 50–53

Follow all water restriction guidelines set by local authorities. Listen to the radio for designated days for watering the lawn etc.

- CONSERVE WATER! Some ways to conserve water:
  – Think of ways water can be reused rather than being poured down the sink (such as using water from the washing up—grey water—to water the garden).
  – Check the house for leaking taps and washers and repair them.
  – Take shorter showers and use toilets with half- and full-flushing options correctly.
  – Turn off taps when brushing your teeth.
  – Wash your car on the grass so it is being watered at the same time (or use a car wash!)
  – Install timers for the sprinklers.

Personally ...

- Ensure you drink plenty of fluids.
- Spend more time inside, out of the sun.
- Wear light-coloured, loose clothing such as clothes made from cotton.
- Reduce outside activity to cooler times of the day.
- Drink plenty of water during strenuous activity.

Ensure animals have water and shelter.

Prim-Ed Publishing   www.prim-ed.com

Emergency procedures

Storms
Pages 54–57

Be prepared before a storm hits:
- Clear away loose objects from around the house.
- Check the roof for loose tiles and clear guttering and downpipes.
- Trim tree branches so they are away from the house.
- Have emergency numbers in an easy to find place.
- Replace batteries in torches and ensure a battery radio is on hand.

As the storm approaches:
- Listen for radio announcements.
- Disconnect electrical appliances.
- Stay inside away from windows.
- If outside, find shelter.

Once the storm has passed:
- Check the house and surrounding trees for damage.
- Stay clear from fallen powerlines and flooded drains.
- Continue to listen to the radio for warnings and advice.

Floods
Pages 54–57

Firstly, find out if your local area is prone to flooding and how severe the last floods were.

As a family, make an action plan for when/if another flood occurs. This must include how the family will be evacuated.

Keep an emergency kit handy that includes:

- first aid kit
- torch with fresh batteries
- portable battery radio
- candles (with waterproof matches)
- emergency contact numbers
- waterproof clothing and shoes
- fresh water
- waterproof bags for valuables

If a flood warning has been announced:
- Listen to the radio for warnings/advice.
- Stack valuables on top of furniture with electrical appliances at the top.
- Secure any objects that may float.
- Ensure poisons and chemicals are in a high, safe place.
- Ensure your neighbours know of the warning.

Emergency procedures

Tornadoes — Pages 58–61

Before a tornado:

- Practise evacuation drills to a designated shelter.
- Prepare disaster supplies — torch with batteries; portable, battery-operated radio; first aid kit and manual; emergency food and water; manual tin opener; essential medicines; cash and credit cards; sturdy shoes.
- Devise a family emergency communication plan in case of separation.

During a tornado:

- Go quickly to designated shelter or a windowless, interior room, hallway, or small room without windows such as a bathroom or built-in wardrobe.
- Stay away from windows and fireplaces.
- Get under a piece of strong furniture and hold on to it.
- Use arms to protect head and neck.
- If in a caravan or car find shelter outside. Lie in a ditch or low-lying area.

After a tornado:

- Help the injured.
- Call for help.
- Stay out of damaged buildings.
- Do not turn on any appliances.
- Listen for emergency information.
- Clean up spilled medicines, bleaches etc.

Bushfires — Pages 62–65

Preparation:

- Make a firebreak around the house. Trim branches and clear roof gutters.
- Store fuel, wood, paint etc. away from the house.
- Keep hoses long enough to reach all parts of the house and garden.

If a bushfire is approaching:

- Phone bushfire brigade to check that they know about the fire.
- Fill baths, sinks, buckets etc. with water and turn off gas and power.
- Remove curtains and move furniture away from windows.
- Hose down walls and plug downpipes, then fill roof gutter with water.

During a bushfire:

- Stay inside until it passes. Wear thick clothing, boots, hat and gloves.
- Put out any fires.
- If the house is alight, move to burnt ground.

If driving:

- Don't drive though a bushfire.
- Stop at a clearing.
- Switch off engine and turn on headlights.
- Close windows and lie down under a woollen blanket.

If on foot:

- Cover exposed skin.
- Find open or already-burnt ground.
- Get into a pond, creek or dam but not a water tank.
- Lie face down in a hollow or under a rock.

Natural Disasters — Prim-Ed Publishing — www.prim-ed.com

Preventative measures

Plagues, epidemics and pandemics

Pages 34–41

The list below provides some measures to follow to help prevent the spread of infectious diseases.

- Cover your face when sneezing or coughing.
- Correctly dispose of soiled tissues immediately.
- Stay away from school or work if suffering from an infectious disease.
- Wash hands thoroughly before handling food.
- Wash hands thoroughly after going to the toilet.
- Use latex gloves when cleaning or handling cuts or abrasions.
- Keep cuts and abrasions covered with a bandage.
- Be aware of stepping on or handling used syringes in public places.
- Don't share items such as toothbrushes or razors.
- Take care when using public toilets; e.g. use a paper seat cover if provided.
- Notify appropriate authorities if vermin are sighted in residential areas; e.g. rats.
- Use insect repellent to protect against mosquitoes and fleas.
- Child and adult immunisation programmes are available for a variety of infectious diseases such as influenza, measles, polio, whooping cough and mumps.

Quiz: Tsunamis — Pages 2–5

1. What is the name for a series of tsunami waves? _____

2. Tick the correct answer.

   (a) The word tsunami means:
   ☐ harbour rise ☐ harbour view ☐ harbour wave

   (b) The distance between waves is the:
   ☐ amplitude ☐ wavelength ☐ circumference

   (c) The height of a wave is the:
   ☐ diameter ☐ amplitude ☐ crest

   (d) The low point of a wave is the:
   ☐ trough ☐ amplitude ☐ basin

   (e) Tsunami waves can travel at speeds up to:
   ☐ 100 km/h ☐ 10 000 km/h ☐ 1000 km/h

3. What phenomenon occurs when:

   (a) the crest of the first tsunami wave hits shore first? _____

   (b) the trough of the first tsunami wave hits shore first? _____

Quiz: The Ring of Fire — Pages 6–9

1. The Ring of Fire marks an area of what type of activity? _____

2. Collisions between the plates of the earth's crust create massive amounts of what? _____

3. Tsunamis occur most frequently in which ocean? _____

4. Which Pacific islands were hit by a tsunami generated by the Aleutian Island earthquake in 1946? _____

5. How long did it take for the tsunami generated by the Great Chilean earthquake in 1960 to reach Japan? _____

6. What major natural disaster occurred in 1883 which resulted in a tsunami in the Indian Ocean? _____

7. Which continents are adjacent to the Ring of Fire?
   - _____
   - _____
   - _____
   - _____

8. Where is the base for the Pacific Tsunami Warning System? _____

NATURAL DISASTERS
Prim-Ed Publishing www.prim-ed.com

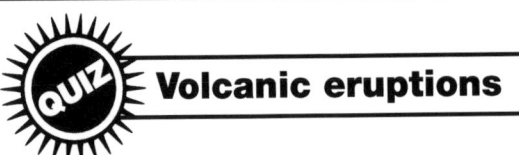 **Volcanic eruptions**   Pages 10–13

1. Name two things which are expelled from a volcano.
   _____
   _____

2. How far beneath the earth's surface can temperatures hot enough to melt rock be found?
   _____

3. What is magma (melted rock) called once it has erupted from a volcano?
   _____

4. A volcanic eruption can trigger a tsunami. True or false?
   _____

5. What do we call a volcano that has stopped erupting altogether?
   _____

6. Most volcanoes are found along the:
   (a) Square of Fire
   (b) Ring of Fire
   (c) Oval of Fire

7. Are all volcanoes mountains?

   | Yes | No |

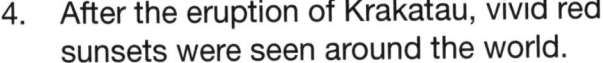 **Volcanic disasters**   Pages 14–17

1. Which volcano caused the greater loss of life – Nevado del Ruiz or Mount Tambora?
   _____

2. In which country will you find Mount Vesuvius?
   _____

3. The eruption of which volcano caused what is thought to be the loudest sound ever heard on earth?
   (a) Mount Pelée
   (b) Mount Vesuvius
   (c) Krakatau

4. After the eruption of Krakatau, vivid red sunsets were seen around the world.

   | True | False |

5. Did more people die from hot gases or starvation after Mount Tambora erupted?
   _____

6. What did most victims of the Mount Pelée eruption die from?
   _____

Earthquakes

Pages 18–21

True or false?

☐ 1. The Modified Mercalli scale measures the power of an earthquake.

☐ 2. A fault is a break in the Earth's crust.

☐ 3. Shock waves from an earthquake are strongest closer to the epicentre.

☐ 4. Scientists can accurately predict when earthquakes will occur.

☐ 5. Earthquakes can be felt over great distances.

☐ 6. Aftershocks may occur for weeks following an earthquake.

☐ 7. The Greeks blamed Mars for earthquakes.

☐ 8. The Hindus believed that six elephants holding up the earth caused earthquakes.

☐ 9. Scientists can predict with some accuracy where earthquakes may occur.

☐ 10. Eighty per cent of earthquakes occur in the 'Ring of Fire'.

The effects of earthquakes

Pages 22–25

1. Is ground shaking during an earthquake stronger on sand and mud, or on bedrock?
   _____

2. What often causes fires after earthquakes?
   _____

3. Where do seiches occur?
   _____

4. What caused the Indian Ocean tsunami in 2004?
   _____

5. Where are landslides likely to occur?
   _____

6. What is the name given to soil which has become so saturated with water that it is no longer strong enough to support the weight of buildings and other structures?

NATURAL DISASTERS   Prim-Ed Publishing   www.prim-ed.com

# Cyclones, hurricanes and typhoons

Pages 26–29

True or false?

1. A cyclone is caused by an area of extreme high pressure and rotating winds around a central eye.
2. The eye has lighter winds and fair weather at its centre.
3. Cyclones may exhibit wind gusts over 300 km/h.
4. Hurricanes can sometimes be called 'anti-cyclones'.
5. Hurricanes are tropical cyclones.
6. There are four categories of hurricanes.
7. The rotating winds of a cyclone in the Southern Hemisphere move in an anticlockwise direction.
8. The rotating winds of a cyclone in the Northern Hemisphere move in a clockwise direction.
9. Cyclones are named 'hurricanes' or 'typhoons' depending on the region.

# Cyclone Tracy

Pages 30–33

1. What was the date that Cyclone Tracy struck Darwin?

2. Where was the eye of the cyclone centred?

3. What was the estimated range of wind speeds during Cyclone Tracy?

4. Write the numbers.
   (a) How many people were killed?
   (b) What percentage of buildings were destroyed or damaged?
   (c) What fraction of the population left Darwin?
   (d) How many days did the airlift last?
   (e) How many people were airlifted from Darwin?
   (f) How many people remained in Darwin?

Prim-Ed Publishing   www.prim-ed.com

Plagues, epidemics and pandemics   **Pages 34–37**

1. Match each word to the best phrase.

    (a) plague •   • contained in one or more communities

    (b) epidemic •   • spread throughout the world

    (c) pandemic •   • usually fatal

2. Circle the century the black death occurred.

    1300s   **1400s**   **1500s**

3. In what year was the world declared 'smallpox free'? _____

4. Was the Spanish flu an epidemic or a pandemic? _____

5. What do the following letters stand for?

    (a) AIDS _____

    (b) HIV _____

The bubonic plague   **Pages 38–41**

1. What name was given to the bubonic plague of the 14th century in Europe?

    _____

2. Name the two animals that spread the plague bacterium.

    _____
    _____

3. List three things that happened to a victim of the plague.

    _____
    _____
    _____
    _____

4. List three unhygienic practices of the time.

    _____
    _____
    _____
    _____

5. List two things people tried to do to prevent the disease.

    _____
    _____
    _____
    _____

NATURAL DISASTERS   Prim-Ed Publishing   www.prim-ed.com

Avalanches, landslides and mudslides Pages 42–45

State yes or no.

1. One hundred thousand avalanches occur each year worldwide.
2. Avalanches are sometimes called 'the white death'.
3. Ninety-five per cent of people caught in an avalanche are caught by a slide triggered by them or by a member of their own party.
4. Avalanches are caused by heavy snowfalls.
5. Motorists on roads can be trapped by avalanches.
6. The United States of America experiences the greatest number of fatalities due to avalanches.
7. Slab avalanches are the most dangerous of the five types of avalanche.
8. Gravity forces large amounts of rock, sand or soil down hills to become a landslide.

Thredbo Ski Resort landslide Pages 46–49

Write short answers.

1. What was the time and date of the Thredbo Ski Resort landslide disaster?

2. What was the volume of the earth, rock and trees which formed the landslide?

3. How many lodges were destroyed and what were their names?

4. How long did it take to discover a survivor?

5. Name two things which were used to sustain Stuart Diver's life until he could be rescued.
   -
   -

6. How many people died altogether in the Thredbo Ski Resort landslide?

Prim-Ed Publishing   www.prim-ed.com

 **Drought**　　　　　　　　　　　　　　　　　**Pages 50–53**

1. Overgrazing is when there is not enough feed to sustain the number of sheep on the land. True or false?

   _____

2. Some effects of drought include unemployment, famine and loss of feed. List four more effects.

   • _____

   • _____

   • _____

   • _____

3. During a drought, crops are damaged and stock (cattle and sheep) numbers may fall. Are consumers affected by the price of these goods rising or falling?

   _____

4. Hot, dry winds can increase the risk of which other natural disaster?

   _____

5. Name two areas in Africa severely affected by drought and starvation.

   _____

 **Storm and floods**　　　　　　　　　　　**Pages 54–57**

1. A flash flood is caused when a storm moves slowly or quickly?

   _____

2. Stay safe during a storm by disconnecting all _____

3. What might people suffer from if the phone they are speaking on during a storm becomes charged from a lightning strike?

   (a) _____

   (b) _____

   (c) _____

4. If the area you live in is prone to flooding, it is important your family has made this type of plan.

   _____

5. What happens to humid warm air when it is given an upward push by surface winds (updraft)?

   _____

 **Tornadoes** **Pages 58–61**

1. Write the correct numbers to answer the questions.

    (a) How tall can 'twisters' grow?
    Over _____ metres

    (b) Wind speeds in tornadoes can reach up to _____ km/h or more.

    (c) The path of destruction may be as long as _____ kilometres.

    (d) The path of destruction may be as wide as _____ kilometres.

    (e) The rating for the most intense tornado on the Fujita Pearson Scale is _____.

    (f) The least dangerous tornado is rated _____ on the Fujita Pearson Scale.

2. Damage during a tornado is not only caused by the tornado itself but also by _____

3. Tornadoes can easily be identified by _____

4. The area of states in the USA where the most intense tornadoes occur is called _____

 **Bushfires** **Pages 62–65**

1. What are the three things necessary for a bushfire to start?
   _____
   _____
   _____

2. The most common natural cause of bushfires is _____

3. Name two ways that bushfires are caused accidentally by people.
   _____
   _____

4. What are people who deliberately light fires called?
   _____

5. What is back-burning?
   _____
   _____
   _____

6. What do firefighters use helicopters for?
   _____
   _____
   _____

7. What trees in Australia contribute to the bushfire problem?
   _____

Natural disasters

Quiz answers

Tsunamis 2–5
1. train
2. (a) harbour wave
   (b) wavelength
   (c) amplitude
   (d) trough
   (e) 1000 km/h
3. (a) run-up
   (b) drawback

Ring of Fire 6–9
1. volcanic and seismic
2. energy
3. Pacific
4. Hawaii
5. almost 24 hours
6. eruption of Krakatoa
7. Australasia; Asia; North America; South America
8. Hawaii

Volcanic eruptions ... 10–13
1. magma (lava), gases, ash, cinders, dust, rock fragments
2. 100 kilometres
3. lava
4. true
5. extinct
6. (b) Ring of Fire
7. no

Volcano disasters 14–17
1. Mount Tambora
2. Italy
3. (c) Krakatau
4. true
5. starvation
6. volcanic ash in the air

Earthquakes 18–21
1. False   6. True
2. True   7. False
3. True   8. False
4. False   9. True
5. True   10. True

The effects of earthquakes 22–25
1. sand and mud
2. broken gas, fuel and power lines
3. in enclosed water; lakes, canals and swimming pools
4. an underwater earthquake
5. in hills and mountains — after earthquakes
6. liquefaction

Cyclones, hurricanes and typhoons 26–29
1. False   6. False
2. True   7. False
3. False   8. False
4. True   9. True
5. True

Cyclone Tracy 30–33
1. 25 December 1974
2. over the airport and northern suburbs
3. between 217 and 300 km/h
4. (a) 65
   (b) 70%
   (c) ³/₄
   (d) 6
   (e) 25 000
   (f) 10 000

Plagues, epidemics and pandemics 34–37
1. (a) usually fatal
   (b) contained in one or more communities
   (c) spread throughout the world
2. 1300s
3. 1980
4. a pandemic
5. (a) Acquired Immune Deficiency Syndrome
   (b) Human Immunodeficiency Virus

The bubonic plague .38–41
1. The Black Death
2. rats and fleas
3. high fever, cough, aching limbs, swellings, vomiting blood, death
4. chamber pots and rubbish emptied in streets, dirt floors, communal water, unwashed food and hands, rarely bathed, dirty clothes
5. wore masks and gloves, hankerchiefs over face, rang church bells, fired cannons, bought spells and charms, placed dead animals in homes, bathed in urine

Avalanches, landslides and mudslides 42–45
1. No   5. Yes
2. Yes   6. No
3. Yes   7. Yes
4. No   8. Yes

Thredbo Ski Resort landslide 46–49
1. 11.35 pm on Wednesday 30 July 1997
2. 2000 cubic metres
3. 2; Carinya, Bimbadeen
4. 55 hours
5. a pipe to circulate warm air around his body; a tube to allow him to slowly sip fluids
6. eighteen

Droughts 50–53
1. True
2. loss of stock, bush or forest fires, dust storms, environmental damage — soil erosion and vegetation loss
3. rising
4. bush or forest fires
5. Ethiopia, Sahel

Storms and floods 54–57
1. slowly
2. electrical appliances
3. electrocution, burns, hearing damage
4. evacuation
5. cools

Tornadoes 58–61
1. (a) over 12 200
   (b) 400
   (c) 80.5
   (d) 1.5
   (e) F–5
   (f) F–0
2. wind-blown debris
3. violently twisting funnels of air
4. 'Tornado Alley'

Bushfires 62–65
1. ignition, fuel, oxygen
2. lightning
3. campfires, fires lit by farmers or caused by machinery
4. arsonists
5. burning the vegetation in front of a bushfire
6. dropping water, gathering information
7. eucalyptus trees

Prim-Ed Publishing   www.prim-ed.com

Natural disasters — Curriculum links

The units of activities throughout this book will help to teach the following literacy and geography curriculum objectives. The final activity in each unit provides either a literacy, geography or cross-curricular activity that covers other curriculum objectives. The curriculum links for these activities are listed on the relevant accompanying pages of teachers notes.

England	English	KS 2	• Read a range of non-fiction texts. • Engage with challenging subject matter. • Obtain specific information through detailed reading.
	Geography	KS 2	• Study a range of places and environments in different parts of the world. • Recognise some physical processes and how these can cause changes in places and environments. • Know about water and its effects on landscapes and people. • Study environmental issues caused by a change in an environment; e.g. drought.
Northern Ireland	Language and literacy	KS 2	• Engage in a wide range of reading activities for a variety of purposes. • Use a variety of reading skills.
	Geography	KS 2	• Study different places, environments and weather conditions. • Investigate the effects of extreme weather conditions and natural disasters, such as flooding, drought, hurricanes, earthquakes and volcanoes, on people and places.
Republic of Ireland	English	5th/6th Class	• Read a more challenging range of reading material, including non-fiction texts. • Use comprehension skills.
	Geography	5th/6th Class	• Become familiar with the distinctive natural features of places in other parts of the world. • Become aware of natural disasters as a cause of famine. • Develop simple understanding of the structure of the Earth; e.g. volcanoes, earthquakes. • Develop simple understanding of some atmospheric features; e.g. weather disasters.
Scotland	English	Level C/D	• Use an increasing range of non-fiction texts. • Read for specific information.
	Society	Level D/E	• Describe how extremes of weather and climate can disastrously affect people and places. • Identify and describe a range of physical features and the processes that formed them; e.g. earthquakes and volcanoes.
Wales	English	KS 2	• Read a range of non-fiction texts. • Read for information from challenging texts. • Read for different purposes, including detailed reading to obtain specific information.
	Geography	KS 2	• Study contrasting localities and environmental change, including what localities are like and the geographical patterns that can be identified.

Prim-Ed Publishing   www.prim-ed.com

Tsunamis

Objectives

- Reads information and answers questions about tsunamis.
- Creates a poster showing essential safety procedures to adopt during a tsunami.

Worksheet information

- Tsunamis are not common; about six major events occur every hundred years.
- To generate a tsunami, a submarine earthquake has to be over 6.75 on the Richter scale.
- The fall in water level which occurs if the trough of the initial wave hits the shore first is called 'drawback'.
- A submarine earthquake is caused when two oceanic plates slide against one another, creating a lot of friction. The plates slip then stick as friction and pressure build up to huge levels. When this pressure is suddenly released, the plates explode apart. This explosion is called an earthquake.
- Tsunamis are not easily detected in deep water because the amplitude of the waves is barely one metre. Seismographs, used to detect earthquakes, and computerised offshore buoys which measure changes in wave height, could alert people to the imminent danger of a tsunami.
- Tsunamis have often been called tidal waves because they look like a huge rushing tide as they approach land. The term is misleading as tsunamis have nothing to do with the tides, tides are caused by the gravitational force of the moon on the sea and waves which are caused by the wind.
- Quiz questions relating to this section may be found on page xviii.
- Emergency procedures relating to this section may be found on page xii.

Answers

page 4

1. (a) 3 (b) 2 (c) 4 (d) 1
2. (a) Tsunami means harbour wave.   (c) Tsunami waves move the entire depth of the ocean.
   (b) A tsunami is a series of waves.   (d) Tsunami waves hold a massive amount of energy.
3 & 4. Teacher check

page 5

Teacher check

Cross-curricular activities

- Pupils create their own tsunamis by:
  (a) dropping a rock into a bowl of water and observing the pattern of waves as they travel from the site of impact.
  (b) gently jolting the bowl of water and observing how forcefully the water pours over the edge on the opposite side of the bowl.
- Using images from library resources and the Internet for inspiration, pupils employ a range of art media to create a representation of a tsunami as it reaches the shore.
- Pupils write a poem about the natural forces which result in a tsunami, considering the power of all phenomena involved rather than the destruction that is caused.

Curriculum links

Page xxvii lists the main literacy and geography curriculum objectives covered by these activities. The final activity in this unit will help to teach the following curriculum objectives.

England	English	KS 2	• Write in a range of forms for a range of purposes and readers.
Northern Ireland	Language and literacy	KS 2	• Write in different formats for a variety of purposes.
Republic of Ireland	English	5th/6th Class	• Write in a variety of genres with a particular purpose and audience in mind.
Scotland	English	Level C	• Write non-narrative texts for a given purpose and audience.
Wales	English	KS 2	• Write for varied purposes.

Prim-Ed Publishing   www.prim-ed.com

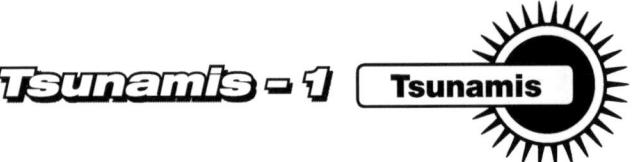

Tsunamis – 1

The word tsunami comes from the Japanese word meaning harbour wave. Tsunamis are a series of waves often referred to as a 'train'. They are caused when a large mass of water is rapidly displaced. This can occur when there is massive movement of oceanic plates at the earth's crust, causing a submarine earthquake.

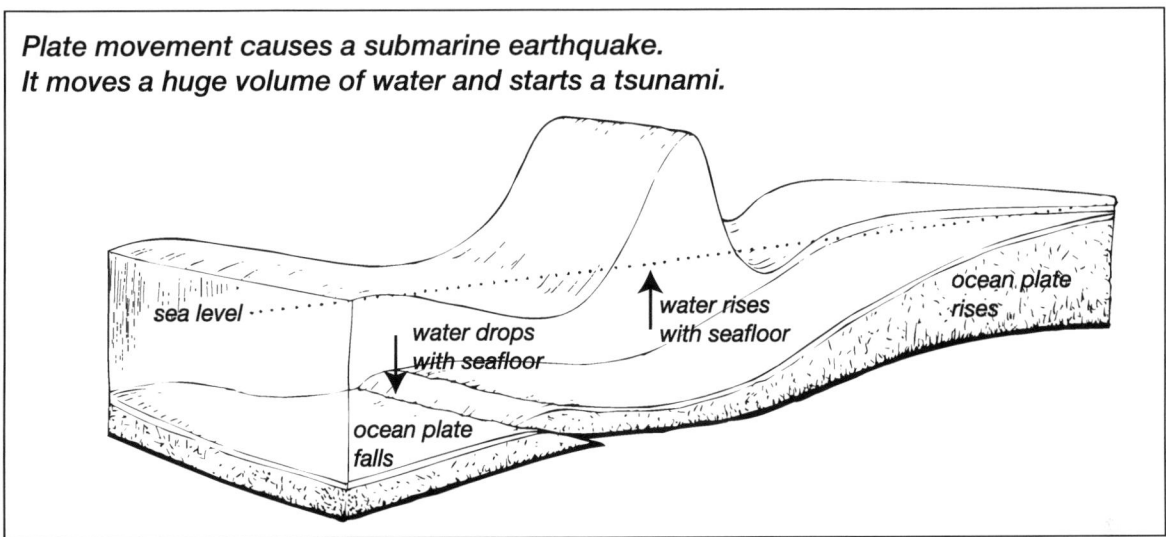

Plate movement causes a submarine earthquake. It moves a huge volume of water and starts a tsunami.

Waves are formed as the mass of displaced water spreads across the ocean. The distance between waves, the wavelength, may be hundreds of kilometres, with the height of each, the amplitude, being only about a metre. But the waves are moving the entire depth of the ocean and hold a massive amount of energy. They can travel at almost 1000 km/h in deep water, ten times faster than a normal wave.

As the tsunami approaches the coast where the depth of the ocean becomes shallow, three things happen:

- the waves slow down,
- the height of the waves increases, reaching up to 30 m,
- the distance between each wave decreases.

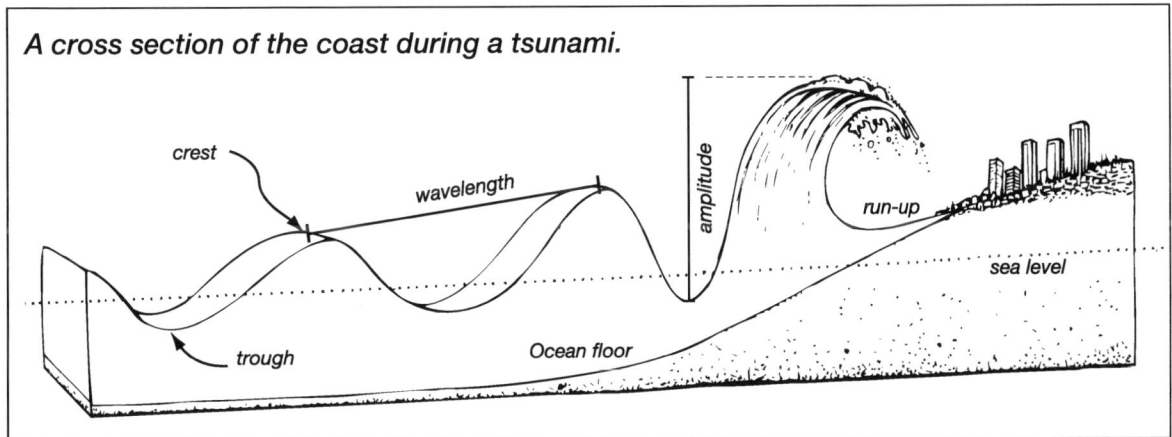

A cross section of the coast during a tsunami.

On the shore, the first visible sign of a tsunami is either a rapid rise or fall in water level. If the crest, or top of the initial wave hits land first, the water level rises causing widespread flooding. This is called the run-up. If the trough, or bottom, hits first, the water level drops as it is sucked into the wave, exposing a vast expanse of land. This is called the drawback. About 15 minutes later, the monstrous waves explode on to the shore, continuing for up to two hours.

Tsunamis

Answer the questions using the text on page 3.

1. Place the events in the correct order by numbering them from 1 to 4.

    (a) A huge mass of water is displaced. ☐

    (b) A submarine earthquake develops. ☐

    (c) A tsunami wave is set in motion. ☐

    (d) Movement between oceanic plates occurs. ☐

2. Match the sentence parts.

    | (a) | Tsunami means | • | • the entire depth of the ocean. |
    | (b) | A tsunami is a | • | • harbour wave. |
    | (c) | Tsunami waves move | • | • a massive amount of energy. |
    | (d) | Tsunami waves hold | • | • series of waves. |

3. Explain these terms in your own words:

    (a) run-up: _____

    _____

    (b) drawback: _____

    _____

4. Draw and label two diagrams.

(a) How the waves look in deep water.	(b) How the waves look close to shore.

Fact file

An earthquake which is too small to generate a tsunami on its own, may trigger an underwater landslide which then causes a tsunami.

NATURAL DISASTERS Prim-Ed Publishing   www.prim-ed.com

Communities throughout the world have procedures for what to do in the event of a natural disaster. Posters remind us of essential things we should or should not do, to ensure the safety of ourselves and those around us.

1. In the boxes, make lists of what you think we should and should not do in the event of a tsunami.

Things we should do	**Things we should not do**

2. Draw an eye-catching, effective poster giving essential advice for what to do in the event of a tsunami. Use the ideas from your lists and the space below to plan your poster.

3. Name some places to display your poster where many people will see it.

Fact file

Animals can give early warning of an approaching tsunami. It is believed that they sense the danger and flee to higher ground.

Tsunamis — Ring of Fire

Objectives

- Reads information and answers questions about the 'Ring of Fire'.
- Learns why the majority of submarine earthquakes and tsunamis occur in the 'Ring of Fire'.

Worksheet information

- Seismic activity refers to earthquakes. Scientists have developed a theory called 'plate tectonics' which explains the geological features and activities occurring at the earth's crust. The extreme temperatures and pressures that exist when oceanic plates collide can result in the formation of chains of violent volcanoes, such as the 'Ring of Fire'.
- There are six major volcanic areas in the 'Ring of Fire'.
- A tsunami may also occur in a fjord, a narrow inlet surrounded by cliffs. A fjord tsunami may be generated when a portion of iceberg breaks, or calves, into the water. The resulting wave pattern is different from that created by a submarine earthquake in an ocean tsunami.
- Quiz questions relating to this section may be found on page xviii.

Answers

page 8

1. Teacher check
2. earthquakes
3. (a) false (b) true (c) false (d) true (e) true
4. Teacher check
5. (a)

   (b) The Ring of Fire is a natural phenomenon.

page 9

Teacher check

Cross-curricular activities

- Pupils draw up a time line of major recorded tsunamis, including a key to illustrate the ocean in which they occurred.
- Pupils collect data from major recorded tsunamis to determine the top five. They may choose their own criteria for determining this; e.g. loss of life, strength of earthquake, greatest distance between earthquake and tsunami.
- Pupils research the tectonic plates in the Pacific region and label them on a map. They research how movement of and collisions between these plates have caused some well-known geographical features.

Curriculum links

Page xxvii lists the main literacy and geography curriculum objectives covered by these activities. The final activity in this unit will help to teach the following curriculum objectives.

England	Geography	KS 2	• Use atlases and maps.
Northern Ireland	Geography	KS 2	• Locate places studied in atlases and on maps.
Republic of Ireland	Geography	5th/6th Class	• Engage in practical use of maps, understand and use common map features; e.g. keys and record directions onto maps.
Scotland	Society	Level C	• Identify world locations on a map.
Wales	Geography	KS 2	• Use maps and locate places using atlases.

NATURAL DISASTERS — Prim-Ed Publishing — www.prim-ed.com

Ring of Fire – 1 — Tsunamis

The **'Ring of Fire'** is an arc marking an area of great volcanic and seismic activity. It is located around the edges of the Pacific Ocean, extending north from New Zealand, along the eastern edge of Asia, east towards the Aleutian Islands, off the coast of Alaska and south along the entire length of both American continents.

The earth's crust is covered with a number of irregular shaped plates which can move and collide with each other, generating massive amounts of energy. This energy can result in the formation of volcanoes and the occurrence of submarine earthquakes. If the earthquake is powerful enough, a tsunami may be generated.

The 'Ring of Fire' lies where the Pacific Plate is colliding with other plates. Although tsunamis are a global phenomenon, they occur most frequently in the Pacific Ocean.

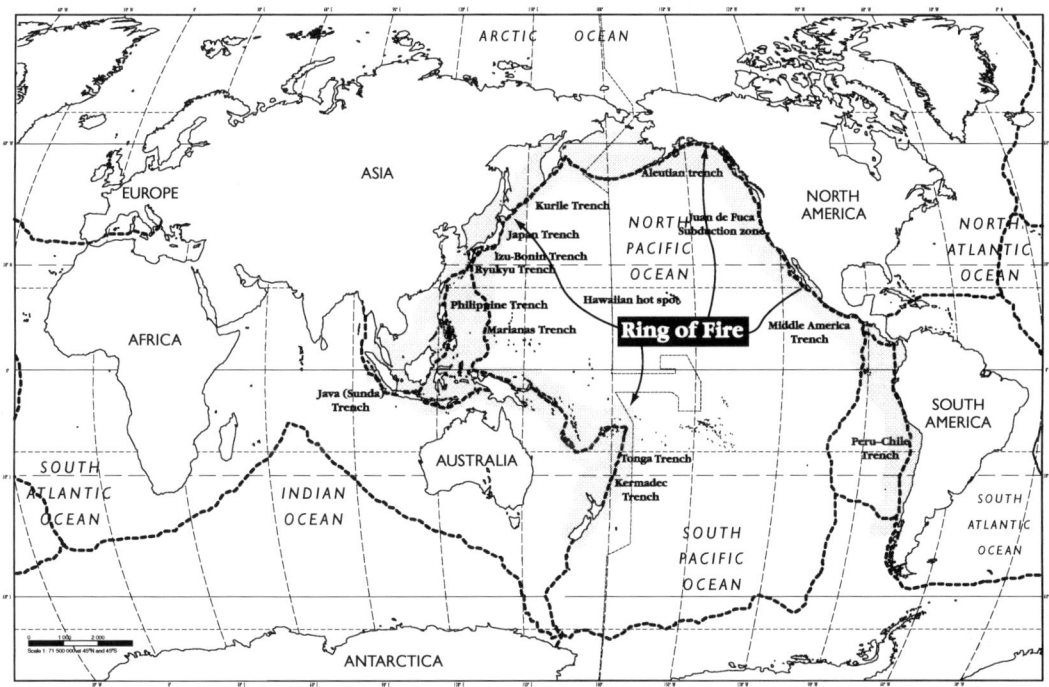

This list shows some of the major 'Ring of Fire' tsunamis caused by earthquakes.

- 1946 – The Aleutian Island earthquake generated a tsunami which badly affected the coast of Alaska and also the Hawaiian islands in the mid-Pacific. Following this disaster, a tsunami warning system was established for countries in the area of the Pacific Ocean.
- 1960 – The Great Chilean earthquake, reaching 9.5 on the Richter scale, caused one of the most devastating tsunamis of the 20th century. Almost 24 hours after the earthquake, the tsunami hit the coast of Japan on the other side of the ocean. 
- 1964 – The Good Friday earthquake in Alaska caused tsunamis which hit areas along the whole length of the North American coast.

The most destructive tsunami on record occurred on Boxing Day 2004, in the Indian Ocean. From Indonesia, Thailand and Malaysia close to the earthquake, to Bangladesh, India, Sri Lanka and the Maldives, thousands of kilometres away, over 300 000 people died. Kenya, Somalia and Tanzania on the east coast of Africa, were also affected. This was the first major tsunami in the Indian Ocean since the eruption of Krakatoa in 1883.

Tsunamis — Ring of Fire – 2

Answer the questions using the text on page 7.

1. Why do you think the Ring of Fire was given its name?

   _____

   _____

2. What natural phenomenon do you think a seismologist studies? ☐

3. Tick **true** or **false**.

   (a) The Ring of Fire is located on the edges of the Indian Ocean. ……… True ◯ False ◯

   (b) The earth's crust is covered with irregular plates. …………………… True ◯ False ◯

   (c) All submarine earthquakes cause tsunamis. ………………………… True ◯ False ◯

   (d) Tsunamis can occur anywhere in the world. …………………………… True ◯ False ◯

   (e) The Richter scale measures the strength of an earthquake. ………… True ◯ False ◯

4. Why do you think a tsunami warning system was established for countries next to the Pacific Ocean but not for those countries adjacent to the Indian Ocean?

   _____

   _____

5. (a) Find these words in the wordsearch. The words may be found in any direction.

Ring of Fire	tsunami	ocean
volcanic	seismic	Aleutian
earthquake	activity	Chile
plate	submarine	Alaska
Pacific	phenomenon	Boxing
energy	global	Day

E	N	E	R	G	Y	T	H	E	R	C	N
A	I	N	G	L	I	O	F	A	I	O	F
R	D	A	Y	O	I	M	K	N	N	R	E
T	I	G	E	B	I	S	A	E	S	L	A
H	S	N	A	A	A	C	M	N	I	N	L
Q	E	I	G	L	L	O	A	H	U	T	E
U	I	X	A	O	N	U	C	R	P	S	U
A	S	O	V	E	F	A	L	E	L	P	T
K	M	B	H	C	I	F	I	C	A	P	I
E	I	P	H	E	N	O	I	M	T	N	A
A	C	T	I	V	I	T	Y	R	E	E	N
N	S	U	B	M	A	R	I	N	E	O	N

   (b) Reading left to right and top to bottom, write the sentence formed from the unused letters.

Fact file

In 1993, seismologists discovered the largest known concentration of volcanoes on the sea floor in the South Pacific – 1133 volcanoes in an area about half the size of Ireland!

Ring of Fire mapping  **Tsunamis**

When we hear of natural disasters around the world, it is helpful to know the exact location of the events and the areas affected by them.

1. Using library resources or the Internet, research any three tsunamis within the Ring of Fire. Record each event.

Tsunami name	Location	Year

2. Label the map with the names of countries, towns and cities affected by the earthquakes and tsunamis.

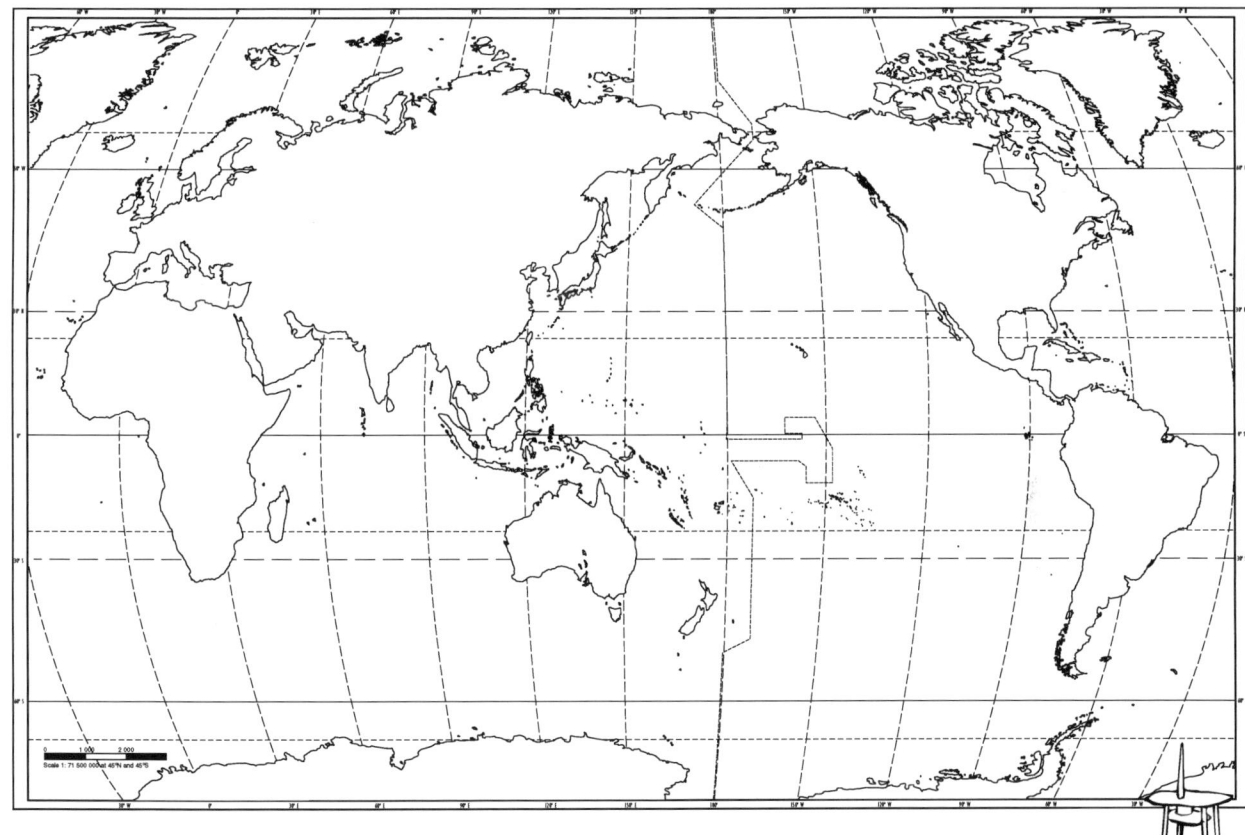

3. (a) Design a coloured key to show:

   earthquake ☐

   tsunami ☐

   direction of tsunami ☐

   (b) Use your key to locate and illustrate the earthquakes and tsunamis on the map.

Fact file

In 1949, the Pacific Tsunami Warning System was established. From a base in Hawaii, modern technology devices help detect earthquakes that may cause a tsunami.

Volcanic eruptions

Objectives

- *Reads information and answers questions about volcanic eruptions.*
- *Conducts a scientific experiment that demonstrates how a volcano erupts.*

Worksheet information

- There are three main groups of volcanoes – shield, cinder cone and composite. Shield volcanoes are dome-shaped and are formed almost entirely from lava flows. Cinder cone volcanoes are cone-shaped and are made almost entirely from fragmented rock ejected from a volcano. Composite volcanoes are also cone-shaped but have been formed from both lava flows and fragmented rock.
- The experiment on page 13 works because when bicarbonate of soda and vinegar mix, a chemical reaction occurs, producing carbon dioxide. The bubbles push the 'lava' up and out of the 'volcano'.
- Quiz questions relating to this section may be found on page xix.
- Emergency procedures relating to this section may be found on page xii.

Answers

page 12

1. Teacher check
2. (a) a volcano expert
   (b) an area which circles the Pacific Ocean, containing most of the world's volcanoes
   (c) a volcano which erupts constantly
   (d) a volcano which has been quiet for some time
   (e) a volcano which has stopped erupting altogether
3. Teacher check
4. lava, gases, ash, cinders, dust, rock fragments
5. Teacher check

page 13

Teacher check

Cross-curricular activities

- Research to create a glossary of terms relating to volcanoes.
- Use coloured map/drawing pins and labels to show the location of some active volcanoes on a map of the world.

Curriculum links

Page xxvii lists the main literacy and geography curriculum objectives covered by these activities. The final activity in this unit will help to teach the following curriculum objectives.

England	Science	KS 2	• Use simple equipment and materials appropriately, make observations and draw conclusions.
Northern Ireland	Science	KS 2	• Record, analyse and present information.
Republic of Ireland	Science	5th/6th Class	• Observe, offer explanations and draw conclusions.
Scotland	Science	Level C	• Make appropriate observations and explain what happens in experiments, drawing on scientific knowledge.
Wales	Science	KS 2	• Use equipment and resources correctly, make observations and draw conclusions.

Prim-Ed Publishing   www.prim-ed.com

Volcanic eruptions – 1

What is a volcano?

A volcano is a place in the earth's surface through which melted rock (magma) and gas erupt. Most volcanoes are found along the 'Ring of Fire', an area which circles the Pacific Ocean. Other places with volcanoes include Hawaii, southern Europe and even under the ocean! Most volcanoes are mountains. The mountain forms when the materials produced during an eruption fall back to earth and build up, creating a cone shape. This process may take thousands of years.

What causes a volcanic eruption?

Far below the earth's surface, it is extremely hot. If you could dig a hole 100 kilometres deep, you would find temperatures hot enough to melt rock. This melted rock is called 'magma'. When hot gases inside the earth build up, they push the magma up towards the surface and eventually it bursts out as a volcanic eruption. Once it has erupted, magma is called 'lava'.

Volcanoes which erupt constantly are called 'active', while those which have been quiet for some time are called 'dormant'. If a volcano stops erupting altogether, it is called 'extinct'. There are about 1500 active volcanoes in the world and many more dormant ones.

What is a volcanic eruption like?

Every volcanic eruption is different. Some volcanoes blast large clouds filled with ash and poisonous gases high into the air and spill hot lava, dust, cinders and rock fragments over large areas. Other volcanic eruptions are quieter, simply expelling flowing lava and gases.

How can you tell when a volcano is going to erupt?

Vulcanologists (volcano experts) use a range of monitoring equipment to help them predict when a volcano might erupt. This is so people in the area can be evacuated in plenty of time. Some of the signs vulcanologists look for include a slight bulge in the sides of a volcano (due to the collecting magma), small earthquakes (caused by rising magma), a temperature increase in the surrounding area and gaseous fumes. But it isn't always possible to tell when a volcano will erupt.

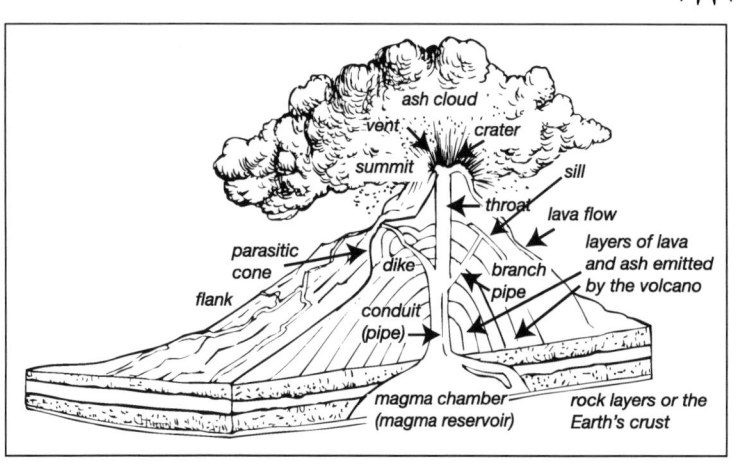

Why are volcanic eruptions so dangerous?

Volcanic eruptions can cause great devastation. It has been estimated that about one million people have been killed by volcanic eruptions over the past 2000 years. Despite this, some people still live near volcanoes. One reason for this is that volcanic ash creates fertile soil for farming. Underground steam caused by volcanoes is also used by people as a source of energy.

But no-one would want to be near a volcano when it erupts! Here are some of the things that can happen during a volcanic eruption.

- *The force of the blast can kill people, plants and animals.*
- *Lava flows can start fires, kill people, plants and animals and bury towns, cities or islands.*
- *Volcanic ash can make jet aircraft engines stall, cause people and animals to suffocate, destroy plants and start fires.*
- *Volcanic bombs (large fragments of rock thrown out of a volcano) can kill people and destroy buildings.*
- *Poisonous gases can kill people and animals if they are breathed in.*
- *Tsunamis, floods, rock falls, mudflows and earthquakes can be triggered.*

Some of the greatest volcanic disasters include the eruptions of Mount Tambora and Krakatau in Indonesia, Mount Pelée in the West Indies and Nevado del Ruiz in Colombia.

Volcanic eruptions — Volcanic eruptions – 2

Use the text on page 11 to answer the questions.

1. In your own words, explain what makes a volcano erupt.

   _____
   _____
   _____
   _____

2. Write a definition for each of these things related to volcanoes.

   (a) vulcanologist _____
   (b) 'Ring of Fire' _____
   (c) active _____
   (d) dormant _____
   (e) extinct _____

3. Would you ever choose to live near a volcano? Yes ◯ No ◯ Explain your answer.

   _____
   _____
   _____

4. List some materials that might be expelled by a volcano during an eruption.

5. What do you think is the biggest danger for humans from a volcanic eruption? Why?

   _____
   _____
   _____
   _____

Fact file

The word 'volcano' comes from 'Vulcan' — the ancient Roman god of fire. He was thought to have made weapons for other gods. The volcanic island of Vulcano, near Sicily, was believed to have been the chimney of his workshop.

Make a volcano — Volcanic eruptions

1. Would you like to see a volcano erupt? Try making your own.
   Make sure you wear old clothes—it can get messy!

   You will need
   - sheets of newspaper (to protect the floor)
   - one A4 sheet of cardboard
   - sticky tape
   - one 'egg cup' (cut from an egg carton)
   - $\frac{1}{2}$ cup of vinegar in a small measuring jug
   - 3–4 tablespoons of bicarbonate of soda
   - red food colouring

   Instructions
   1. Place the newspaper on the floor.
   2. Make a cone from the cardboard with a gap at the top for the egg cup to fit snugly into. It might take you a few attempts to make this work. When you are happy with the cone, tape it together. Cut off any excess card from the bottom so the cone will stand up by itself.
   3. Place the cone on the newspaper.
   4. Add the bicarbonate of soda and a few drops of the red food colouring to the egg cup and mix.
   5. Place the egg cup into the top of the 'volcano' cone. Carefully pour the vinegar into the egg cup.
   6. Stand back and watch your volcano erupt!

2. Answer these questions after the experiment.
   (a) Write what you observed.

   (b) Write why you think this might have happened.

   (c) Find out from your teacher or the Internet why the volcano 'erupted'. Write the explanation below. How close is it to your explanation?

   Fact file
   The volcano Stromboli, in Italy, has been erupting without a break for more than 2000 years!

Volcanic eruptions — Volcanic disasters

Objectives

- Reads information and answers questions about some of the world's worst volcanic disasters.
- Plans and writes a legend about a volcano.

Worksheet information

- The top 10 most deadly volcanic eruptions are as follows: Mount Tambora (1815), Krakatau (1883), Mount Pelée (1902), Nevado del Ruiz (1985), Unzen, Japan (1792), Laki, Iceland (1783), Kelut, Indonesia (1919), Galunggung, Indonesia (1882), Mount Vesuvius (1631 and 79 AD).
- Quiz questions relating to this section may be found on page xix.

Answers

page 16

1. (a) fact
   (b) opinion
   (c) opinion
   (d) fact
2. (a) Mount Tambora
   (b) Volcanic ash from the eruption blocked out sunlight, causing cooler conditions around the world.

3.

Volcano	Date of eruption	No. of deaths	Causes of deaths
Mount Tambora	1815	92 000	hot gases, rock and other volcanic materials, starvation
Krakatau	1883	36 000	tsunami, volcanic gases, ash
Mount Pelée	1902	29 000	volcanic ash, lava flow
Nevado del Ruiz	1985	23 000	lahars, volcanic material
Mount Vesuvius	79 AD	3300	ash, rocks, mud, lava

4. (a) He was underground.
   (b) Crops were destroyed.

page 17

Teacher check

Cross-curricular activities

- Label a diagram of a volcano.
- Create volcano shape poems.
- Draw an impression of Vulcan, the Roman god of fire, whom volcanoes were named after.

Curriculum links

Page xxvii lists the main literacy and geography curriculum objectives covered by these activities. The final activity in this unit will help to teach the following curriculum objectives.

England	English	KS 2	Use ICT-based reference materials and write in a range of forms.
Northern Ireland	Language and literacy	KS 2	Read electronic texts on the Internet and write in different formats.
Republic of Ireland	English	5th/6th Class	Find information through the use of IT and write in a variety of genres.
Scotland	English	Level C/D	Use a search engine and develop imaginative writing.
Wales	English	KS 2	Use ICT-based reference materials and write imaginatively.

Volcanic disasters – 1 — Volcanic eruptions

Some volcanic eruptions have caused terrible destruction and loss of life. Read about some of the world's worst volcanic disasters.

Mount Tambora, Indonesia
Date: 1815   Deaths: 92 000

The Mount Tambora eruption has been the most powerful to date in modern history. It was so violent that about 150 cubic kilometres of melted rock was blasted out of the volcano. The heat from the eruption also caused a whirlwind, which destroyed villages and plant life, including crops. Approximately 10 000 people were killed immediately from hot gases, rock and other materials ejected from the volcano and about 82 000 more died later, mostly from starvation.

The Mount Tambora eruption sent a huge cloud of volcanic ash into the atmosphere, which blocked out sunlight and caused cooler conditions in countries around the world; 1816 became known as 'the year without a summer' in some areas because of this.

Krakatau, Indonesia
Date: 1883   Deaths: 36 000

The explosion of the volcanic island of Krakatau (also known as 'Krakatoa') in 1883 is thought to have been the loudest sound ever heard on earth. The huge volume of ash and lava produced even formed some new islands! It is believed that no-one was killed from the initial explosion, but tens of thousands of people died as a result of the tsunami triggered by the eruption. A lesser number also died from volcanic gases and ash. In addition, about 160 villages were devastated.

For several months after the eruption, vivid red sunsets were seen around the world. This was due to sunlight reflecting from the volcanic dust in the atmosphere.

Mount Pelée, Martinique (West Indies)
Date: 1902   Deaths: 29 000

Prior to its 1902 eruption, Mount Pelée was thought to be extinct. The eruption destroyed the nearby city of Saint Pierre, killing all but two inhabitants. One lived on the outskirts of the city and the other was a prisoner who was in an underground jail cell!

Most of Mount Pelée's victims died from the volcanic ash in the air. Others were killed when a lava flow struck nearby villages.

Nevado del Ruiz, Colombia
Date: 1985   Deaths: 23 000

When Nevado del Ruiz erupted, the snow at its summit melted and created mudflows (lahars) that swept down the volcano. By the time they reached the bottom, they were up to 40 metres thick and were travelling up to 50 kilometres per hour! Almost all of the people who died were from one town, Armero, which was completely covered in volcanic material.

Mount Vesuvius, Italy
Date: 79 AD
Deaths: 3 300

The eruption of Mt Vesuvius in 79 AD is one of the most famous volcanic eruptions. It completely buried the towns of Pompeii, Herculaneum and Stabiae, preserving buildings, bodies and artefacts in the lava layers.

According to an eyewitness, Mount Vesuvius erupted with great violence. Flames soared high into the sky and an enormous black cloud blocked out the sun. After three days, a layer of ash, rocks, mud and lava had covered the three towns.

Mount Vesuvius has erupted many times since 79 AD, including an occasion in 1631 in which 3500 people were killed.

Volcanic eruptions — Volcanic disasters – 2

Use the text on page 15 to answer the questions.

1. Tick fact or opinion.

		fact	opinion
(a)	The explosion of Krakatau is thought to have been the loudest sound ever heard on earth.		
(b)	The most frightening volcanic eruption to have witnessed would have been that of Mount Vesuvius.		
(c)	Nevado del Ruiz will never erupt again.		
(d)	The Mount Tambora eruption has so far been the most powerful eruption in modern history.		

2. (a) The eruption of which volcano caused 'the year without a summer'? _____

   (b) Explain why it was called this. _____

3. Complete the table.

Volcano	Date of eruption	Number of deaths	Causes of deaths

4. Explain why you think:

   (a) the prisoner in Saint Pierre might have survived the eruption of Mount Pelée.

   (b) people may not have had enough to eat after the eruption of Mount Tambora.

Fact file
The country with the most volcanoes is Indonesia. More than 80 have erupted in its history.

NATURAL DISASTERS — Prim-Ed Publishing   www.prim-ed.com

Volcanic legends — Volcanic eruptions

Throughout history, people have tried to explain natural events like volcanic eruptions through legends. It is only in more recent times that science has been able to explain how and why volcanoes erupt.

Try writing your own legend that explains the eruption of a volcano. It can be one of the volcanoes described on page 15 or an imaginary one.

1. Begin by using the Internet or other resources to research some traditional legends about volcanic eruptions.

   (Hint: If you are using an Internet search engine, try typing in 'volcanic eruptions legends' or 'volcanoes legends').

   List some of the interesting characters or ideas from your research.

   Characters

   Ideas

2. Use the ideas from Question 1 to help you write a plan for your legend.

   - Name and location of volcano: _____

   - How will your legend explain why volcanoes erupt? _____

   Characters

   Plot

   Beginning

   Middle

   End

3. Write your legend on a separate sheet of paper. Add a suitable title and one or more illustrations.

   Fact file
   The temperature of the hottest lava can be around 1200 °C!

Prim-Ed Publishing   www.prim-ed.com

NATURAL DISASTERS

Earthquakes

Objectives

- Reads information and answers questions about earthquakes.
- Completes a crossword.

Worksheet information

- Pupils need to understand that the Richter and the Modified Mercalli scales give very different information about earthquakes. The first is a measure of the power or magnitude of the earthquake, and the second its effect on people and property and that, therefore, location is an important factor; for example, an earthquake occurring in a sparsely populated area wouldn't cause the damage of one of the same magnitude in a city. In Question 3 on page 20, the pupils are required to think about the type of property that could be damaged in an earthquake and the dangers it could pose.
- Quiz questions relating to this section may be found on page xx.
- Emergency procedures relating to this section may be found on page xiii.

Answers

page 20

1. (a) Earthquakes are caused by rock shifting along a fault in the Earth's crust.
   (b) It is the area directly above where the movement occurs.
   (c) The Richter scale
   (d) It is used to record the damage done by an earthquake since this depends on factors other than magnitude.
2. (a) The Greeks thought that the god Poseidon was responsible for earthquakes.
   (b) Teacher check
   (c) Aristotle believed that earthquakes were caused by hot air escaping from the centre of the Earth.
3. Teacher check

page 21

1. *Across*:
   1. epicentre, 5. scientist, 6. heat, 8. underground, 10. and, 11. measure, 13. philosopher

   Down:
   1. earthquake, 2. crust, 3. time, 4. less, 7. power, 9. danger, 12. SOS
2. Teacher check

Cross-curricular activities

- Pupils research the 12 levels identified on the Modified Mercalli scale. These could be illustrated and made into a class display.
- Map locations of earthquakes throughout the world.
- Work in small groups to formulate an action plan to deal with an earthquake near the school.

Curriculum links

Page xxvii lists the main literacy and geography curriculum objectives covered by these activities. The final activity in this unit will help to teach the following curriculum objectives.

England	Geography	KS 2	• Use appropriate geographical vocabulary.
Northern Ireland	Geography	KS 2	• Use precise subject specific vocabulary.
Republic of Ireland	English	5th/6th Class	• Experience a growing elaboration and sophistication in the use of vocabulary.
Scotland	Society	Level E	• Use appropriate specialist vocabulary.
Wales	Geography	KS 2	• Use and extend their geographical vocabulary.

Earthquakes – 1

Earthquakes

Scientific knowledge might be advancing at a tremendous rate, but one thing we still can't do is control nature! Natural causes are responsible for many phenomenon, including earthquakes.

What is an earthquake?

An earthquake is the shaking of the ground caused by rock shifting along a fault, which is a break in the Earth's crust where the plates of rock meet.

Earthquakes can release stress that has been building up within the rock for hundreds of years. The plates of rock may move apart (A), push together (B), or slide against each other (C). The movement, possibly lasting only a few seconds, may be felt over very long distances and cause great damage and loss of life.

Before people understood what caused earthquakes, there were many different theories. The Greeks blamed Poseidon, the god of the sea. Many others thought the Earth rested on the backs of very large animals and earthquakes occurred when the tired or restless animals moved. The Hindus believed eight elephants held the Earth, while in South America, the animal was a whale. Aristotle, the famous Greek philosopher, was more scientific; he believed earthquakes were caused by hot air trying to escape from the centre of the Earth.

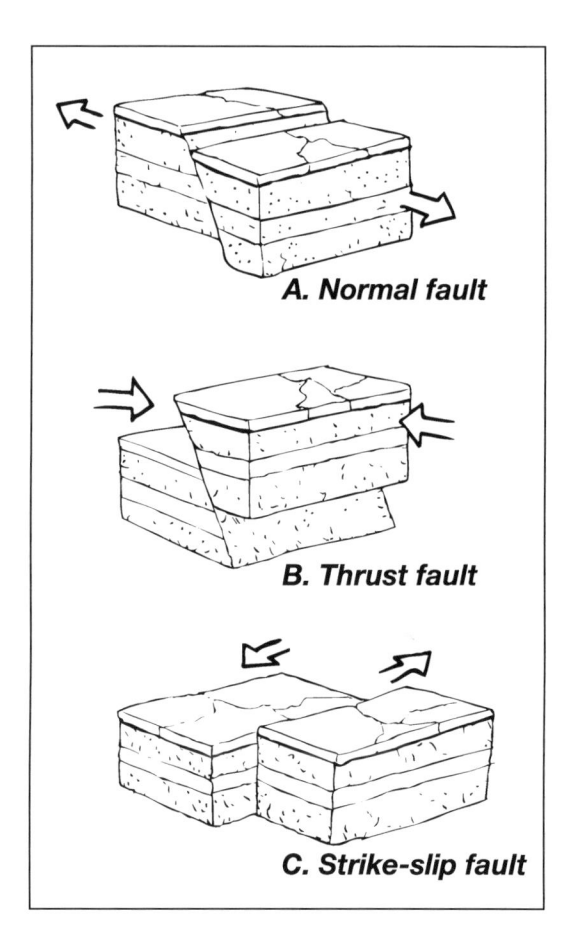

A. Normal fault

B. Thrust fault

C. Strike-slip fault

Measuring earthquakes

A scale for measuring the power of earthquakes from 1 to 10 was developed in 1935 by Charles Richter. This scale is still used, although it was modified in 1977.

Another method for measuring the damage and effect an earthquake has on people is the Modified Mercalli scale. This scale measures from I (just detectable by experienced observers) to XII (major catastrophe, objects thrown in the air and vision distorted by vibrations).

Earthquakes have an epicentre, which is directly above the area where the underground movement occurred. The epicentre is the point on the Earth's surface from which the shock waves radiate. The shock waves are strongest closer to the epicentre and decrease as they move away. It is common for an earthquake to be followed by a series of after-shocks of less intensity, which may continue for weeks. These can cause considerable damage to structures already weakened or damaged by the original quake and can make rescue operations even more difficult and dangerous.

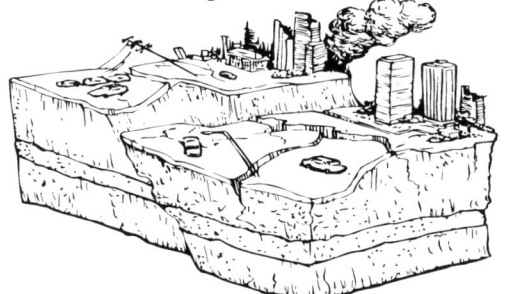

Predicting earthquakes

Scientists can now predict with some accuracy where earthquakes are likely to occur but are less able to tell when they will happen. An area around the Pacific Ocean, known as the Ring of Fire, is expected to be where 80 per cent of the world's future earthquakes will occur.

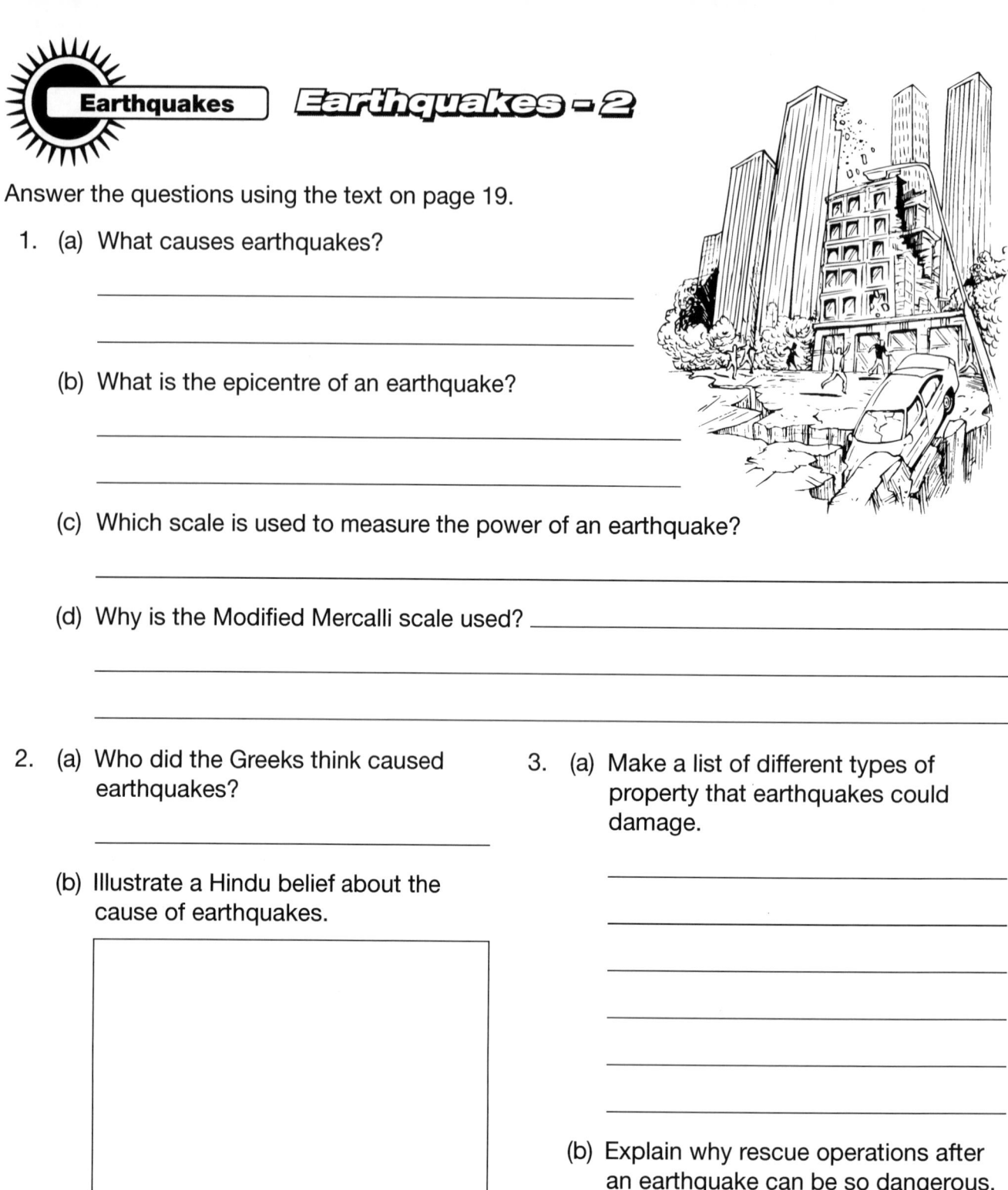

Earthquakes – 2

Answer the questions using the text on page 19.

1. (a) What causes earthquakes?

   _____

   _____

   (b) What is the epicentre of an earthquake?

   _____

   _____

   (c) Which scale is used to measure the power of an earthquake?

   _____

   (d) Why is the Modified Mercalli scale used? _____

   _____

   _____

2. (a) Who did the Greeks think caused earthquakes?

   _____

   (b) Illustrate a Hindu belief about the cause of earthquakes.

   [   ]

   (c) What did Aristotle believe caused earthquakes?

   _____

   _____

   _____

3. (a) Make a list of different types of property that earthquakes could damage.

   _____

   _____

   _____

   _____

   _____

   (b) Explain why rescue operations after an earthquake can be so dangerous.

   _____

   _____

   _____

   _____

Fact file

The most powerful earthquake ever recorded was in Chile in 1960. It measured 9.5 on the Richter scale. More than 2000 were killed, 3000 injured and 2 million made homeless.

Earthquake crossword

Earthquakes

1. Complete the crossword. You will find most of the words in the information you read about earthquakes on page 19, but there are a few others to test your thinking skills.

Across
1. Where shock waves start. (9)
5. A person who may study earthquakes (9)
6. Opposite of 'to cool' (4)
8. Earthquakes occur here (11)
10. In addition (3)
11. The Richter scale is used to … magnitude (7)
13. Aristotle was one (11)

Down
1. A vibration in the Earth (10)
2. Earthquakes occur in the Earth's … (5)
3. Earthquakes last a short … (4)
4. The opposite of more (4)
7. The Richter scale measures the … of earthquakes (5)
9. Rescuers must be aware of it (6)
12. A distress message (3)

2. Write crossword clues of your own for these words.

(a) fault

_____

(b) scale

_____

(c) Mercalli

_____

(d) vibration

_____

Fact file

The combined force of earthquakes in one year is 100 000 times more powerful than the atomic bomb which destroyed the city of Hiroshima in Japan.

Earthquakes — The effects of earthquakes

Objectives

- Reads information and answers questions about the effects of earthquakes.
- Records and uses information to write and illustrate a newspaper report.

Worksheet information

- Pupils will need to be familiar with the layout and language used in newspaper reports, particularly those reporting major events; for example, the headline, the human interest story, the official reaction or comment and the photograph with a suitable caption. They will benefit from opportunities to read and analyse newspaper reports before attempting to write one of their own.
- Quiz questions relating to this section may be found on page xx.

Answers

page 24

1. (a) Answers may include: The destruction resulting from an earthquake depends on the power of the earthquake, measured on the Richter scale, and its location including factors of population density, buildings and other structures and the type of soil. (Sand and mud magnify shaking more than bedrock.)
   (b) Landslides can cover roads, railways and buildings and sweep whole villages away.
   (c) Lake Sarez was formed when an earthquake caused a massive landslide which formed a dam across the river.
2. (a) Fires can be caused by broken gas, fuel and power lines.
   (b) Broken water pipes can make fighting some fires difficult.
3. (a) Seiches are rhythmic movements or sloshing in enclosed water.
   (b) They may cause dams to break, topple buildings and trees and cause local flooding.
   (c) The water movement was caused by a major earthquake in Lisbon, Portugal.

page 25

1. Teacher check
2. Teacher check

Cross-curricular activities

- Research avalanches; definition, causes, effects and history.
- Dramatise 'an earthquake in the classroom', after some class or small-group discussion about what would be likely to happen and how pupils would feel and act during and immediately after it occurred.
- Discuss possible reasons why today there is concern for the safety of people living in the valley below Lake Sarez and write a newspaper report alerting people to the potential disaster.

Curriculum links

Page xxvii lists the main literacy and geography curriculum objectives covered by these activities. The final activity in this unit will help to teach the following curriculum objectives.

England	English	KS 2	• Write in a range of forms for a range of purposes and readers.
Northern Ireland	Language and literacy	KS 2	• Write in different formats for a variety of purposes.
Republic of Ireland	English	5th/6th Class	• Write in a variety of genres with a particular purpose and audience in mind.
Scotland	English	Level C	• Write non-narrative texts for a given purpose and audience.
Wales	English	KS 2	• Write for varied purposes.

NATURAL DISASTERS — Prim-Ed Publishing www.prim-ed.com

The effects of earthquakes – 1 — Earthquakes

Earthquakes have had a profound effect on the Earth. They have been responsible for permanent land features like scarps and surface ruptures, as well as the destruction caused by ground-shaking movements, landslides, liquefaction, tsunamis, fires and seiches.

Ground-shaking movements can damage buildings and other structures and result in death and injury, depending on the magnitude of the earthquake and its location. Sand and mud magnify ground shaking more than bedrock and also result in more damage. A powerful earthquake affecting Iran in 1990, resulted in 40 000 to 50 000 deaths, with 60 000 injures and a half a million people left homeless.

Landslides occur in hilly regions and can cover roads and railway lines, destroy property and result in many casualties. In Tajikistan, in central Asia, in 1911, a huge earthquake (8–9 on the Richter scale) caused a landslide which created a dam higher than the Empire State Building across the river. Lake Sarez, which is over 60 kilometres long, formed behind the dam. There were comparatively few deaths because of the area's isolation.

Liquefaction occurs when water-saturated soil becomes so fluid it can no longer support the weight of buildings and other constructions. This occurred on the Caspian Sea, following the 1990 earthquake in Iran. The soil lost its strength and structures sank or were spread apart by the liquefied soil.

Tsunamis are sea waves that can be caused by earthquakes beneath the ocean. They travel very fast and are dangerous because as they approach the coast, they are forced to slow down and increase drastically in height. The Indian Ocean tsunami on 26 December 2004 was caused by an underwater earthquake. It was among the deadliest disasters of modern times, killing well over 300 000 people.

Fires occur because earthquakes break gas, fuel and power lines. Fighting fires is often difficult because water pipes are also broken. This was a significant factor in the fires that destroyed so much of San Francisco after the terrible earthquake in 1906. Although the earthquake only measured 7.7, there were 3000 deaths and 524 million dollars worth of damage to property.

Seiches are like small tsunamis in enclosed water, like lakes, canals and even swimming pools. The rhythmic movements or sloshing of the water may cause dams to break, knock houses down, tip over trees or result in some local flooding. Following the earthquake, tsunami and fires which killed more than a third of the population of Lisbon, Portugal in 1755, people were amazed to see water moving in canals as far away as Scotland and Sweden.

Earthquakes — The effects of earthquakes - 2

Answer the questions using the text provided on page 23.

1. (a) Explain why some earthquakes are more destructive than others.

   _____
   _____
   _____
   _____
   _____
   _____

   (b) Why are landslides so dangerous?

   _____
   _____
   _____
   _____

   (c) Explain how Lake Sarez was formed.

   _____
   _____
   _____
   _____

2. (a) What causes fires following earthquakes in urban areas? _____
   _____

   (b) Why are these fires often so difficult to extinguish? _____
   _____

3. (a) What are seiches? _____
   _____

   (b) Why are they dangerous? _____
   _____

   (c) Explain why the water in Scottish and Swedish canals was sloshing about in 1755.
   _____
   _____

   Fact file
   A mudslide disaster following an earthquake in the Paez River in south-western Colombia caused 1000 deaths on 6 June 1994.

Newspaper report — Earthquakes

1. Consider the effects of an imaginary earthquake near where you live and write notes to complete the information table below.

Time	Date	Location

Description of earthquake	People's reactions

Damage to property	Injuries sustained

Emergency services	Rescue operations

2. Use your information as a source for a newspaper report. Include an attention-grabbing headline, an eyewitness account and an appropriate illustration. Consider how you want the readers to feel and think.

Fact file

The most devastating earthquake in modern times was in north-east China in 1976. It measured 8.3 on the Richter scale. Some 240 000 people died and 164 000 were seriously injured.

Prim-Ed Publishing   www.prim-ed.com

NATURAL DISASTERS

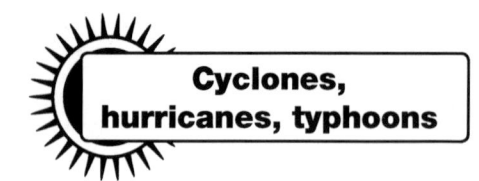

Cyclones, hurricanes, typhoons

Cyclones, hurricanes and typhoons

Objectives
- Reads information and answers questions about cyclones, hurricanes and typhoons.
- Completes a crossword using words from a text about cyclones, hurricanes and typhoons.

Worksheet information

- Pupils will need an atlas and a red, yellow and orange pencil or fine-point marker to complete Question 1 on page 28. Pupils need to ensure that they draw their spirals rotating in a clockwise direction for those in the Southern Hemisphere and in an anticlockwise direction in the Northern Hemisphere. Arrows on the spirals should be used to indicate the rotation direction. As shown on the right.

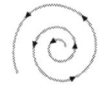

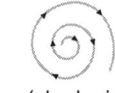

Northern Hemisphere (anticlockwise)   Southern Hemisphere (clockwise)

- Quiz questions relating to this section may be found on page xxi.
- Emergency procedures relating to this section may be found on page xiii.

Answers

page 28

1. Teacher check (Spirals should be anticlockwise in the Northern Hemisphere and clockwise in the Southern Hemisphere.)

2. (a) Tropical cyclones are given a name because many storms may build up in the same area at the same time. Names assist forecasters to easily communicate information about a specific storm to the public.

   (b) Teacher check

page 29

[crossword solution with answers including: scale, depression, rotation, hurricane, anticlockwise, name, gusts]

Cross-curricular activities

- Pupils research to find out if their name has ever been given to a tropical cyclone.
- Pupils draw 'before' and 'after' pictures depicting their school or local area before and after a cyclone, hurricane or typhoon has hit.
- Hunrakan was the name the Indians of Guatemala gave to the god of stormy weather. Investigate and list the names of other gods associated with nature and weather.

Curriculum links

Page xxvii lists the main literacy and geography curriculum objectives covered by these activities. The final activity in this unit will help to teach the following curriculum objectives.

England	Geography	KS 2	Use appropriate geographical vocabulary and use atlases and maps.
Northern Ireland	Geography	KS 2	Use precise subject specific vocabulary and locate places studied in atlases and on maps.
Republic of Ireland	English/ Geography	5th/6th Class	Experience a growing elaboration and sophistication in the use of vocabulary and engage in practical use of maps.
Scotland	Society	Level C/E	Use appropriate specialist vocabulary and identify world locations on a map.
Wales	Geography	KS 2	Use and extend their geographical vocabulary and locate places using atlases.

Cyclones, hurricanes and typhoons – 1

Cyclones, hurricanes, typhoons

What is a cyclone?

In meteorological terms, a cyclone is 'an area of extreme low pressure which is characterised by winds rotating around a central calm *eye*'.

The rotating winds of a cyclone move in a clockwise direction in the Southern Hemisphere and an anticlockwise direction in the Northern Hemisphere.

The 'eye' is a roughly circular area consisting of lighter winds and fair weather found at the centre of a severe tropical cyclone. The winds at the centre of a cyclone are the most destructive and may extend over one hundred kilometres from the centre of the cyclone. Wind gusts may reach a speed of over 280 km/h. A cyclone often produces large amounts of rain which can cause flooding, as well as destructive winds.

Often a number of storms may be present in the same area at the same time. For this reason, tropical cyclones are usually given a name to allow forecasters to communicate forecasts, watches and warnings about a specific storm to the general public.

Tropical cyclones may be classified as:

- *tropical depressions* (with winds up to 61 km/h)
- *tropical storms* (with winds from 62–118 km/h)
- *hurricanes* (with winds from 119 km/h or more).

Cyclones can be found south of the Equator — more specifically in the south-west Pacific Ocean west of 160° E or in the south-east Indian Ocean east of 90° E or in the south-west Indian Ocean.

'Anti-cyclones'—hurricanes—can be found north of the Equator.

What is a hurricane?

A hurricane is a type of tropical cyclone. These usually occur in the North Atlantic Ocean, the north-east Pacific Ocean, east of the International dateline or in the South Pacific Ocean east of 160° E.

Hurricanes form over the warm waters of the Equator. The rotating winds of a hurricane move at at least 119 km/h. Huge amounts of rain, low air pressure, thunder and lightning occur in association with a hurricane. The winds rotate in an anticlockwise direction. Hurricanes can often travel from the ocean to the land where they can cause massive destruction.

Hurricanes are classified according to the Saffir-Simpson Scale:

- *category 1:*   winds 119–153 km/h
- *category 2:*   winds 154–177 km/h
- *category 3:*   winds 178–209 km/h
- *category 4:*   winds 210–249 km/h
- *category 5:*   winds over 250 km/h

HURRICANE

spiral rainbands
a series of long spiralling bands of rain clouds

eye
calm centre

eyewall
a wall of dense thunder clouds surrounding the eye where the strongest winds occur

What is a typhoon?

A typhoon is a tropical cyclone which forms in the north-west Pacific Ocean west of the International dateline and in the China Seas.

'Cyclone' is the generic term which includes both hurricanes and typhoons.

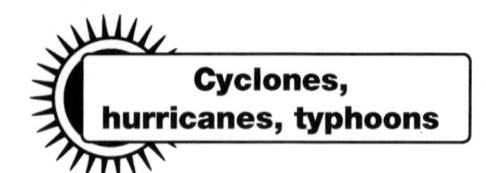

Cyclones, hurricanes and typhoons – 2

Cyclones, hurricanes, typhoons

Use the text on page 27 to answer the questions.

1. Use the world map to draw coloured spirals where cyclones, hurricanes and typhoons occur. Ensure that your spirals are rotating in the correct direction.

KEY: Cyclones – red; Hurricanes – yellow; Typhoons – orange

Fact file
In 1970 a cyclone hit Bangladesh, killing 500 000 people — making it the worst natural disaster of the 20th century!

2. Answer the questions.

(a) Why are tropical cyclones given a name?

(b) Why do you think hurricanes need to be classified?

Natural Disasters — Prim-Ed Publishing   www.prim-ed.com

Cyclonic crossword

Cyclones, hurricanes, typhoons

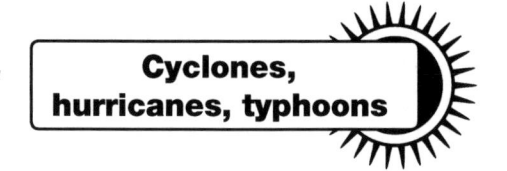

Complete the crossword using the information from page 27.

Across

2. Categories of hurricanes are given according to the Saffir-Simpson …
5. A tropical … has winds up to 61 km/h.
6. The winds of a cyclone form a …
9. A … is a type of tropical cyclone.
10. Cyclones in the Northern Hemisphere move in an … direction.
14. Tropical cyclones are given a … to distinguish one from another.
15. Wind … in a cyclone may reach a speed of over 280 km/h.

Down

1. Hurricanes are given a … depending on their wind speed.
3. The wind and rain from cyclones causes a lot of …
4. Cyclones in the Southern Hemisphere move in a … direction.
7. A hurricane is a … cyclone.
8. The calm, central area of a cyclone is called an …
11. A cyclone in the China Seas is called a …
12. … is the term which includes hurricanes and typhoons.
13. Cyclones are created by an area of low … with winds rotating around a central **eye**.

Fact file

Hurricanes are powered by the heat energy released by the condensation of water vapour. The sea's surface temperature must be above 26.5 °C.

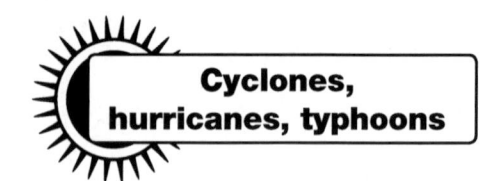

Cyclones, hurricanes, typhoons — Cyclone Tracy

Objectives

- Reads information and answers questions about Cyclone Tracy.
- Designs a building able to withstand cyclonic conditions.

Worksheet information

- If possible, pupils should complete the cloze passage on page 32 without referring to the text on page 31, to assess what they have learnt. After an initial attempt, pupils may return to the text to complete answers they are uncertain about. Answers to this section may be corrected by swapping work with a partner.
- Pupils may wish to research information about methods of construction, building materials etc. before completing the activity on page 33. They may also wish to conduct experiments about the strongest shapes to use, the use of crossbeams in specific places to strengthen wall frames or the best methods to construct the foundations of their buildings. Pupils may wish to build a model of their structure and evaluate the design process.
- Quiz questions relating to this section may be found on page xxi.

Answers

page 32

1. (a) Christmas Day (b) 1974
   (c) midnight (d) 7 am
   (e) 217 (f) 300
   (g) airport (h) northern suburbs
   (i) Forty-nine (j) sixteen
   (k) Seventy (l) hundreds
   (m) millions (n) communication
   (o) power (p) water
   (q) sewerage (r) military
   (s) 25 000 (t) 10 000
   (u) law and order (v) defence forces

2. (a) Darwin had not previously been severely affected by a cyclone for many years, and
   (b) it was Christmas Eve
3. Teacher check

page 33

Teacher check

Cross-curricular activities

- Pupils write a sad poem or diary entry which depicts their feelings after having lost their home and belongings in a cyclone.
- Pupils devise a cyclone survival kit, listing and explaining the items that they would include.
- Pupils research and sketch types of buildings used in different weather conditions, such as extreme heat or cold.

Curriculum links

Page xxvii lists the main literacy and geography curriculum objectives covered by these activities. The final activity in this unit will help to teach the following curriculum objectives.

England	Design and technology	KS 2	• Communicate design ideas, bearing in mind the uses and purposes for which the product is intended.
Northern Ireland	Science and technology	KS 2	• Combine designing skills with knowledge and understanding in order to present solutions.
Republic of Ireland	Science	5th/6th Class	• Communicate their design plan using sketches.
Scotland	Technology	Level C	• Think up and communicate a design plan.
Wales	Design and technology	KS 2	• Consider function, safety and reliability when developing design ideas for products.

Cyclone Tracy – 1

Cyclones, hurricanes, typhoons

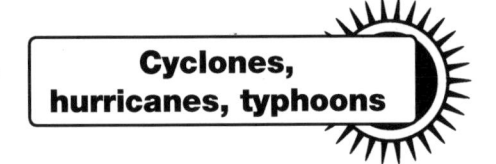

The disaster

A small tropical depression in the Arafura Sea was detected by the Australian Bureau of Meteorology on 20 December 1974, 700 kilometres north-east of Darwin. It was not thought to pose a threat to the Australian coastal city as it began to move slowly in a south-west direction. However, it intensified as it moved close to Bathurst Island on 23 and 24 December and then turned sharply towards Darwin.

The cyclone passed directly over the city between midnight and 7 am on Christmas Day, pounding it with torrential rain and wind gusts between 217 and 300 kilometres per hour. The eye of the cyclone was centred over the airport and the northern suburbs. Massive destruction led to flying debris and glass from buildings being hurled everywhere.

Forty-nine people in the city were killed and another sixteen perished at sea. Many more were injured. When the cyclone had passed, it was estimated that seventy per cent of Darwin's homes had been destroyed or suffered structural damage, at a cost of hundreds of millions of dollars. All important community services, including communication, power, water and sewerage were destroyed.

Warnings were issued about the approach of the cyclone but because Darwin had not been affected by a severe cyclone for many years, and also because it was Christmas Eve, Darwin residents were caught unawares. The poor design of the buildings is also thought to have contributed to the devastation.

The clean-up

Relief measures commenced under the leadership of Major-General Alan Stretton, the Director-General of the Natural Disasters Organisation, on Christmas night. An airlift consisting of both military and civilian aircraft helped many residents to leave the city. Those who were able to, left by road. Three-quarters of the population of Darwin had left within several weeks. The airlift, which began on Boxing Day and lasted for six days, evacuated more than 25 000 people to southern cities. Fewer than 10 000 people remained.

Emergency committees were organised to deal with accommodation, clothing, food, communications, law and order, sanitation and health and social welfare. The responsibility for cleaning up the city rested mainly with the defence forces.

The results

Due to the devastation of Darwin by Cyclone Tracy on Christmas Day in 1974, building codes for construction were upgraded and the social aspects of disaster planning were given greater attention.

Darwin has now been rebuilt into a thriving Australian city again.

Cyclones, hurricanes, typhoons

Cyclone Tracy – 2

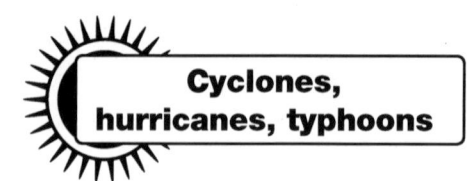

Use the text on page 31 to answer the questions.

1. Complete the cloze.

   Cyclone Tracy struck Darwin on _____ (a) in _____ (b). Between _____ (c) and _____ (d) wind gusts of between _____ (e) and _____ (f) kilometres per hour buffeted the city and dumped torrential rain. The eye of the cyclone was directly over the _____ (g) and _____ (h). _____ (i) people were killed in the city and _____ (j) people died at sea. Many more were injured. _____ (k) per cent of the buildings were destroyed or suffered structural damage. Damage was estimated at _____ (l) of _____ (m) of dollars. All community services were destroyed, including _____ (n), _____ (o), _____ (p) and _____ (q).

   An airlift by civilian and _____ (r) aircraft evacuated more than _____ (s) people to southern cities. Fewer than _____ (t) people remained in Darwin. Emergency committees were organised to deal with accommodation, clothing, food, communications, _____ (u), sanitation and health and social welfare. The _____ (v) were responsible for most of the clean-up.

2. Give two reasons why the residents of Darwin were not unduly concerned about the warnings issued about Cyclone Tracy.

3. What do you think it means by the phrase 'the social aspects of disaster planning were given greater attention'?

   _____

   _____

   _____

   Fact file
   The anemometer at Darwin Airport was destroyed after recording wind gusts of 217 km/h during Cyclone Tracy.

Cyclone shelter design

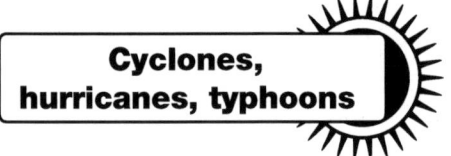

Cyclones, hurricanes, typhoons

After Cyclone Tracy struck Darwin in 1974, the Northern Territory Electricity Commission investigated the possibility of developing a reliable, cyclone-proof power supply for the city.

Engineering consultant company Sinclair Knight Mertz was appointed to design, engineer and act as project manager. The plant utilised two gas turbine generators and distillate fuel. The operation of the plant is fully automatic and by remote control from Stokes Hill Power Station. The casing of the turbine house was tested by propelling the equivalent of a standard 4 x 2 timber beam into it at cyclonic wind speeds.

Use the table below to design a house capable of surviving a cyclone. Ensure that the house is able to provide its residents with the basic necessities — communication to the outside world, water, food, sanitation and shelter. You may be as creative as you wish.

Shape and construction method	Materials for construction
	external walls
	roof
	internal walls
Power source and location	**Sanitation**
Water supply	**Food supply**
Communication	**Sketch your design**
Other factors	

Fact file

In the six months following Cyclone Tracy, access to Darwin was only possible by people who possessed a permit.

Plagues, epidemics and pandemics

Objectives

- Reads information and answers questions about plagues, epidemics and pandemics.
- Completes word study activities based on the theme.

Worksheet information

- Infectious diseases can be spread in a variety of ways. These include: through the air when a person coughs or sneezes out water droplets, from soiled items, from direct or indirect contact with another person, via skin or mucous membrane, saliva, blood, body secretions and urine and through sexual contact.
- Not all diseases become epidemics or pandemics. First and foremost, the germs need to be transferred to new hosts to keep reproducing. In small populations, everyone can contract the disease in a short time and the disease can die out. History has shown that a population needs to be over 250 000 before an epidemic can develop. This is the reason epidemics were not recorded until cities grew to this size.
- Pupils will need access to a dictionary to complete Question 2 on page 36 and Question 1 (b) on page 37.
- Quiz questions relating to this section can be found on page xxii.
- Preventative measures relating to this section can be found on page xvii.

Answers

page 36

1. An epidemic is a lot of cases of illness or disease that spread rapidly in one or more communities, while a pandemic spreads throughout the world.
2. (a) made dirty or impure
   (b) the state of being deprived of water or other fluids
   (c) when a person's appearance has been spoiled or deformed
   (d) to put into or take into the body
   (e) the inability to voluntarily move muscles
3. Teacher check

page 37

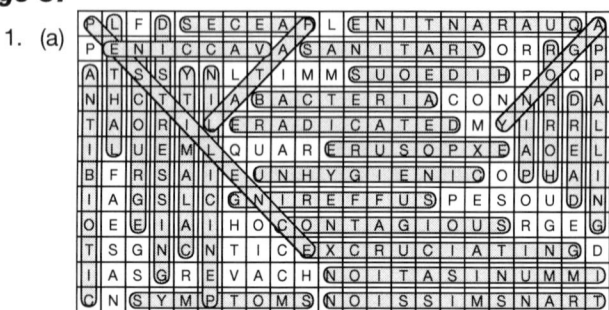

1. (a) [word search grid]
   (b) Teacher check
   (c) pestilence and penicillin
   (d) Teacher check
   (e) bacteria, calamity, penicillin, sanitary, unhygienic

Cross-curricular activities

- Pupils can use the Internet and nonfiction material to find out about infectious diseases that have been and still could be epidemics, such as: measles, tuberculosis (TB), diphtheria, whooping cough (pertussis), mad cow disease (or BSE, bovine spongiform encephalopathy), SARS (Severe Acute Respiratory Syndrome), typhus, typhoid fever, hepatitis B and rubella (German measles).
- Investigate the differences between the appearance and behaviour of a grasshopper and a locust.
- Discuss the use of modern hygiene practices used in the home, school and medical facilities to help prevent the spread of infectious diseases.

Curriculum links

Page xxvii lists the main literacy and geography curriculum objectives covered by these activities. The final activity in this unit will help to teach the following curriculum objectives.

England	English	KS 2	Use vocabulary with more complex meanings.
Northern Ireland	Language and literacy	KS 2	Acquire and develop a vocabulary.
Republic of Ireland	English	5th/6th Class	Experience a growing elaboration and sophistication in the use of vocabulary.
Scotland	English	Level D	Use specialist vocabulary from other curricular areas.
Wales	English	KS 2	Extend and enrich vocabulary through activities that focus on words and their meanings.

Plagues, epidemics and pandemics – 1

A *plague* is any serious disease, usually fatal, which spreads very quickly and is highly contagious. An *epidemic* is a lot of cases of an illness or disease, not necessarily fatal, that spread rapidly over a short time in one or more communities. A *pandemic* is when an epidemic spreads throughout the world.

Throughout history, and even into the present, the world has experienced some terrifying plagues, epidemics and pandemics. Some of these are outlined below.

The Black Death

A deadly plague called the 'Black Death' killed more than 75 million people in Europe and Asia between 1347 and 1351. The medical term for it is the bubonic plague. Victims first developed high fever, a cough and aching limbs. Swellings called 'buboes' soon appeared in the neck, armpits and groin areas. These grew in size and were red at first before turning black. Victims vomited blood. The swellings continued to expand until they eventually burst, with death occurring soon after.

At the time, people did not know the cause of this horrifying disease—being bitten by fleas who had lived on rats infected by the bubonic plague.

The Spanish flu

The Spanish flu was the most common name given to the influenza pandemic of 1918 to 1919. It occurred at the end of World War I, and with a death count between 20 and 40 million, killed more people than the war itself. Victims suffered the usual flu symptoms of coughing, fever, chills, muscle aches, breathing difficulties etc. But this strain was extremely severe. Although it was known flu was spread by breathing in contaminated water droplets, doctors could do little for sufferers.

Smallpox

In 1980, the WHA (World Health Assembly) declared the world free of smallpox due to a successful worldwide vaccination programme. Until then, epidemics of smallpox had killed and disfigured millions of people. Victims were left with deep pockmarks on their skin from pussy lumps erupting. It was spread by contact with the skin lesions or water droplets from the sufferer's airways.

Cholera

Cholera is a violent disease with the possibility of death occurring within 12 to 24 hours. In the 1800s, it became the world's first pandemic. Victims experienced excessive diarrhoea, severe muscular cramps, vomiting and fever. Dehydration turned victims' skin black, blue and wrinkled. Unknown at the time, cholera was spread by ingesting water, food or other material contaminated by the faeces of a sufferer.

Polio

Polio can be a mild disease, but in a small percentage of sufferers it can cause death, paralysis of limbs or total paralysis. Major polio epidemics have been recorded since the late 19th century; for example, in the USA in 1916, 27 000 people suffered paralysis and 6000 died. Polio mainly affects children under five and is spread through contact with the bowel movements of a sufferer (for instance, children's nappies). Since polio vaccine was developed in the 1950s, the disease has disappeared except for in a few third world countries.

AIDS

Epidemics of AIDS (Acquired Immune Deficiency Syndrome) have resulted in 20 million deaths since the first case was reported in 1981. It is caused by HIV (Human Immunodeficiency Virus) which weakens a person's ability to fight infection. Most commonly, sufferers develop severe lung infections, tumours and, eventually, death. It is spread by body fluids in situations such as drug addicts sharing needles that have infected blood or a mother with HIV breastfeeding her baby.

Locust plagues

A non-medical type of destructive plague that has occurred since ancient times is caused by an insect called a locust, which is a type of grasshopper. Massive swarms of locusts can cause severe damage to cereal, vegetable, fruit and fodder crops as locusts can eat their own weight in food every day. This results in huge financial losses, as well as in famine, as has occurred in parts of Africa.

Plagues, epidemics and pandemics – 2

Use the text on page 35 to answer the questions.

1. Briefly describe the difference between an epidemic and a pandemic.
   _____
   _____

2. Use the text and a dictionary to write a definition for each word.

   (a) contaminated _____

   (b) dehydration _____

   (c) disfigured _____

   (d) ingesting _____

   (e) paralysis _____

3. Use keywords and phrases to complete the table below.

	Plague, epidemic or pandemic	Symptoms experienced	Cause
Black Death			
Spanish flu			
Smallpox			
Polio			
AIDS			
Cholera			
Locusts			

Fact file

The Spanish flu was so contagious that authorities in some parts of the world made it illegal to cough, spit or sneeze in public.

Plague of words

Plagues, epidemics and pandemics

1. In the wordsearch below are words associated with plagues, epidemics and pandemics.

    (a) Highlight each word as you find it.

    (b) Tick each word if you understand its meaning. Use a dictionary to check the meaning of any unknown words.

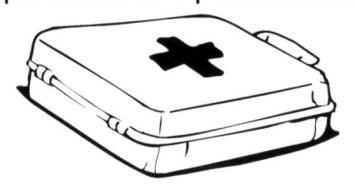

agony	dread	horror	sanitary
antibiotic	eradicated	immunisation	scourge
appalling	excruciating	lethal	suffering
bacteria	exposure	pain	symptoms
calamity	faeces	pestilence	transmission
contagious	fatal	penicillin	unhygienic
distressing	hideous	quarantine	vaccine

P	L	F	D	S	E	C	E	A	F	L	E	N	I	T	N	A	R	A	U	Q	A
P	E	N	I	C	C	A	V	A	S	A	N	I	T	A	R	Y	O	R	R	G	P
A	T	S	S	Y	N	L	T	I	M	M	S	U	O	E	D	I	H	P	O	Q	P
N	H	C	T	T	I	A	B	A	C	T	E	R	I	A	C	O	N	N	R	D	A
T	A	O	R	I	L	E	R	A	D	I	C	A	T	E	D	M	Y	I	R	R	L
I	L	U	E	M	L	Q	U	A	R	E	R	U	S	O	P	X	E	A	O	E	L
B	F	R	S	A	I	E	U	N	H	Y	G	I	E	N	I	C	O	P	H	A	I
I	A	G	S	L	C	G	N	I	R	E	F	F	U	S	P	E	S	O	U	D	N
O	E	E	I	A	I	H	O	C	O	N	T	A	G	I	O	U	S	R	G	E	G
T	S	G	N	C	N	T	I	C	E	X	C	R	U	C	I	A	T	I	N	G	D
I	A	S	G	R	E	V	A	C	H	N	O	I	T	A	S	I	N	U	M	M	I
C	N	S	Y	M	P	T	O	M	S	N	O	I	S	S	I	M	S	N	A	R	T

(c) Which two words in the list above are not in alphabetical order?

(d) Draw neat lines through each word to show the syllable breaks.

   For example: **a/gon/y**

(e) Which words have four syllables?

Fact file

During the polio epidemic of the 1950s, parents kept their children away from playgrounds, pools and cinemas in case they caught the disease.

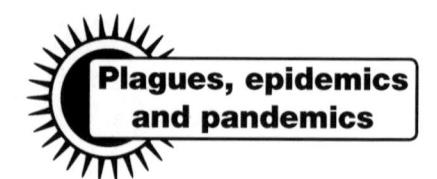

Plagues, epidemics and pandemics
The bubonic plague

Objectives
- Reads information and answers questions about the bubonic plague.
- Completes a plan for an emotive poem about experiencing the bubonic plague.

Worksheet information
- Formats for the specific types of poems mentioned on page 41 may need to be revised with the pupils before commencing the activity; for example:

  A cinquain is a five-line poem that describes something.
  - Line 1 has 1 word with two syllables to describe the topic.
  - Line 2 has 2 words or 4 syllables to describe the title.
  - Line 3 has 3 words or 6 syllables to describe what the topic does.
  - Line 4 has 4 words or 8 syllables to describe the feeling or mood.
  - Line 5 has 1 word or 2 syllables with a similar meaning to the topic.

  An acrostic poem uses a keyword with the letters in the word used as beginnings of words in each line of the poem.

  A syllable poem describes a keyword. Each line has an extra syllable added.

  Ballads often use couplets (rhyming pairs of words). There are usually four lines in a verse, which sometimes have a repeated line.

  Lyric poems express a poet's feelings about a particular topic, feeling or situation. They often use rhyming couplets, are short in length and do not have verses.

- Quiz questions relating to this section can be found on page xxii.

Answers

page 40

1. (a) grotesque (b) dormant
   (c) excruciating or agonising
   (d) diminish (e) communal
2. The victim's body was covered in black blotches.
3. Answers will vary but may include: victims experienced excruciating deaths, victims' appearance was grotesque, death occurred violently and quickly, people had no idea what caused it or how to prevent it
4. It was caused by a bacterium, commonly carried by rats. Fleas that lived on the rats became infected and passed it on when they bit again.
5. The filthy living conditions at the time were ideal for rats and fleas and unhygienic practices readily spread germs.
6. Water was hard to collect and was saved for drinking and cooking.
7. (a) false (b) true (c) false (d) true (e) false (f) false

page 41

Teacher check

Cross-curricular activities
- Pupils could write a diary entry for a survivor of the black death.
- With the foresight of knowing how the disease is spread, pupils could design protective clothing to visit a plague victim.
- Discuss the use of modern hygiene practices used in the home compared to medieval times.

Curriculum links

Page xxvii lists the main literacy and geography curriculum objectives covered by these activities. The final activity in this unit will help to teach the following curriculum objectives.

England	English	KS 2	• Use a range of writing forms, including poems.
Northern Ireland	Language and literacy	KS 2	• Use a variety of writing forms, including poems and experiment with poetic forms.
Republic of Ireland	English	5th/6th Class	• Write in a wide variety of genres, including poetry.
Scotland	English	Level C	• Write poetry.
Wales	English	KS 2	• Use imaginative forms of writing, including poems.

NATURAL DISASTERS   Prim-Ed Publishing   www.prim-ed.com

The bubonic plague – 1

Plagues, epidemics and pandemics

The **bubonic plague** is a disease which has probably been more feared than any other. We talk about it as if it was in the past, but the plague is still with us today. Fortunately, there is now a cure, if it is diagnosed in time.

The worst outbreak of the plague occurred in the 14th century in Europe, when more than one-third of the entire population was killed. Victims experienced such excruciating deaths that those who had not yet caught it lived in absolute dread.

This plague became known as the 'Black Death'. Victims first developed high fever, a cough and aching limbs. Swellings called 'buboes' soon appeared in the neck, armpits and groin areas. These grew in size and were red at first before turning black. Victims vomited blood. The swellings continued to expand until they eventually burst, with death occurring soon after. From the victim's first symptoms, to his or her agonising death, took as little as three or four days. These facts, along with the grotesque appearance of the victim, made this plague especially terrifying. What made matters even worse was that people had no idea what caused it.

We now know the plague is caused by a bacterium, commonly carried by rats. Fleas live on rats and become infected when they bite the rat and ingest its contaminated blood. The fleas can then infect other rats or humans when they bite again.

Understanding the living conditions at the time will give a clear picture of just how easily this disease spread. In the 14th century, living conditions were filthy for both rich and poor, compared with today. Houses did not have toilets. People used chamber-pots to relieve themselves and emptied these, along with other rubbish, into the street. Many houses had dirt floors. People shared communal water and handled unwashed food with unwashed hands. They rarely had a bath as water was hard to collect and was saved for drinking and cooking. Clothes were not often washed or changed. People were unaware that these unhygienic practices spread germs. These conditions were also ideal for rats and fleas and people accepted living with them as a normal part of life.

People tried all sorts of things to prevent the disease. Some people wore masks and gloves when visiting plague houses. Handkerchiefs were dipped in scented oils to cover the face, towns rang church bells and fired cannons to drive the plague away, people bought spells and charms, they placed dead animals in their houses in the hope the smell would drive the plague away and even bathed in human urine! None of these 'cures' worked, of course. The only time the disease diminished was in winter, as fleas are dormant then.

So high was the death rate that there weren't enough people to bury the dead. Bodies were piled into pits or thrown into rivers, which added to the spread of germs and disease. A severe shortage of workers occurred as another result of the high death rate. Whole towns, villages and farms were abandoned and food production fell, leading to starvation in many parts of Europe.

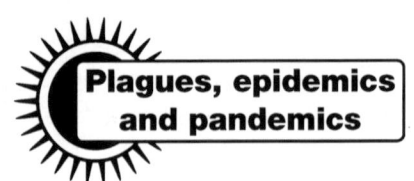

Plagues, epidemics and pandemics
The bubonic plague – 2

Use the text on page 39 to answer the questions.

1. Find a word (or words) in the text to match each meaning.

   (a) unnatural in appearance

   (b) not active

   (c) extremely painful

   (d) to become smaller

   (e) shared by several people

2. Why do you think the plague was called the 'Black Death'?

3. Briefly explain why this plague was so terrifying.

4. What caused this plague?

5. What effect did the living conditions have on the plague?

6. Why did people rarely bathe?

7. Answer true or false.

   (a) The black death killed one-quarter of the population of Europe.
   True / False

   (b) People took as little as three or four days to die from the plague.
   True / False

   (c) The rich did not get the plague.
   True / False

   (d) The disease eased off in winter.
   True / False

   (e) Graves were dug for everybody.
   True / False

   (f) There is still no cure for the bubonic plague.
   True / False

Fact file

The beak-like mask worn by people visiting plague victims was filled with spices and vinegar-soaked cloth to hide the terrible smell of death and decay.

Plague poetry

Plagues, epidemics and pandemics

Did you know that the simple children's rhyme 'Ring around the rosies' actually describes the bubonic plague?

Ring around the rosies	(Rosies refers to the rosy pink rash associated with plague)
A pocket full of posies	(Posies of flowers to mask the foul odours of death)
A tishoo, a tishoo	(Sneezing is a symptom of the plague)
We all fall down	(Falling down means to die)

Can you imagine what it would be like to have lived during epidemics of the bubonic plague? Read through the information on page 39 again and discuss your feelings in a group. Use the results of the discussion to complete the questions below, which will help you to write an emotive poem about the plague known as the Black Death.

1. What type of poem will you write? The examples below would be most suitable for writing an emotive poem. Tick the type you will choose.

   cinquain ☐   acrostic ☐   syllable poem ☐

   short ballad ☐   short lyric ☐   other ☐ _____

2. What is the title of your poem? _____

3. What are some words and phrases you could use in your poem?

Words to describe images	Words to describe feelings	Words to describe smells

4. After you have written a draft copy and published your poem, practise reading it out loud, using your voice to add to the emotion. Then read it to a partner or small group.

Fact file

The majority of soldiers in an invading army in the 13th century were struck down with plague. Survivors catapulted bodies of the victims into the city.

Avalanches, landslides and mudslides

Objectives

- Reads information and answers questions about avalanches, landslides and mudslides.
- Completes a plan for a poem about an avalanche.

Worksheet information

- Pupils may need to be reminded about formats for specific types of poems before commencing page 45; for example:

– A shape poem looks like the topic being written about. – An acrostic poem uses a keyword with the letters in the word used as beginnings of words in each line of the poem. – A syllable poem describes a keyword. Each line has an extra syllable added. – A string poem also describes a keyword and follows the pattern: *Line 1* — The keyword is written 3 times. *Line 2* — Visual description *Line 3* — Describes the size *Line 4* — Describes what it does/they do. *Line 5* — Describes something interesting. *Line 6* — The keyword is written 3 times again.	– An haiku is a Japanese poem made up of 3 lines: *Line 1* has 5 syllables and states where it is. *Line 2* has 7 syllables and states what it is or what it is doing. *Line 3* has 5 syllables and states when or what is being felt or what is happening. – A cinquain is a five-line poem that describes something: *Line 1* has 1 word or 2 syllables to describe the topic. *Line 2* has 2 words or 4 syllables to describe the title. *Line 3* has 3 words or 6 syllables to describe what the topic does. *Line 4* has 4 words or 8 syllables to describe the feeling or mood. *Line 5* has 1 word or 2 syllables with a similar meaning as the topic.

- Pupils may wish to attempt more than one type of poem about avalanches.
- Quiz questions relating to this section may be found on page xxiii.
- Emergency procedures relating to this section may be found on page xiv.

Answers

page 44

1. (a) the white death
   (b) changes in temperature, a loud noise, vibrations or movements in rocks or stones in and around the snow
   (c) triggered by themselves or a member of their party
   (d) starting zone, track, runout zone
   (e) answers may include: loose snow avalanches, ice fall avalanches, roof avalanches, cornice fall avalanches, slab avalanches
   (f) slab avalanches
   (g) 1 000 000; France, Austria, Switzerland, Italy; 150; thousands
2. Teacher check

page 45

Teacher check

Cross-curricular activities

- Pupils create sound effects to resemble an avalanche moving downhill.
- Pupils draw a series of sketches which depict the movement of an avalanche. Join these to create a small book which, when 'flipped', shows an avalanche which actually moves, much as a cartoon does.
- Pupils use body movements to imitate skiers trying to outrun an avalanche.

Curriculum links

Page xxvii lists the main literacy and geography curriculum objectives covered by these activities. The final activity in this unit will help to teach the following curriculum objectives.

England	English	KS 2	Use a range of writing forms, including poems.
Northern Ireland	Language and literacy	KS 2	Use a variety of writing forms, including poems and experiment with poetic forms.
Republic of Ireland	English	5th/6th Class	Write in a wide variety of genres, including poetry.
Scotland	English	Level C	Write poetry.
Wales	English	KS 2	Use imaginative forms of writing, including poems.

Avalanches, landslides and mudslides – 1

Avalanches, landslides, mudslides

Avalanches occur in the mountainous regions of the world over 1 000 000 times each year. The 'white death', as they are sometimes called, occur as snow on a slope adjusts to the pull of gravity. They are a naturally occurring phenomenon.

Avalanches may be triggered by changes in temperature, a loud noise, vibrations or movements in rocks or stones around or in the snow. But often they are the result of human disturbance: 95% of people who are caught in an avalanche are caught by a slide triggered by them or a member of their party.

Every year, more than 150 lives are lost due to avalanches, while thousands more are partly buried or injured. Injuries may be to skiers, snowboarders or motorists trapped on a road. The number of fatalities increases each year as more people are attracted to leisure-time activities. France, Austria, Switzerland and Italy—who all have alpine areas—experience the greatest number of avalanches and loss of life.

Avalanches have a 'starting zone', continue down a slope along a 'track', then fan out to finally settle in the 'runout zone'.

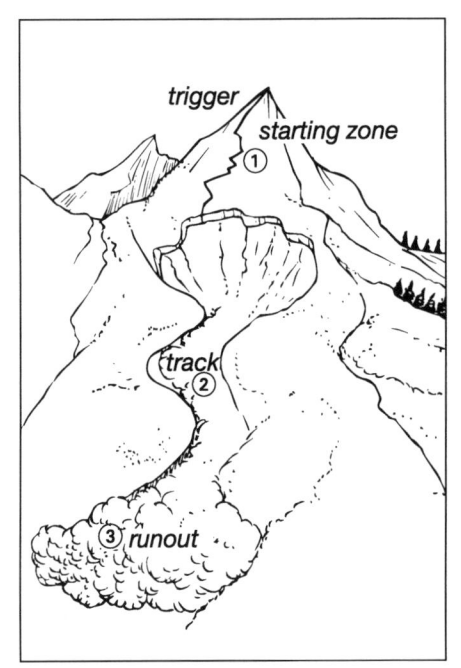

Slab avalanche

Snow avalanches may take a number of forms:
- *loose snow avalanches (sluff)*
  These occur at the surface in new or wet spring snow. This type of avalanche often begins at one point and spreads out as it moves. These are not usually considered very dangerous.
- *ice fall avalanches*
  These occur when a glacier encounters a steep drop. Large parts fall off as the glacier slowly moves downhill under the force of gravity.
- *roof avalanches*
  Snow slides from roofs as the inside of a house or cabin warms up. These can be deadly!
- *cornice fall avalanches*
  These occur when cornices break from the sides of mountain ridges which are sheltered from the wind. The 'ocean wave'-like structures form when winds move snow from slopes on one side of a ridge to deposit it on the other.
- *slab avalanches*
  These are the most dangerous as they can be difficult to see or avoid. Massive amounts of snow are released as one unit.

Landslides usually involve the movement of large amounts of soil, rock, mud or sand or a combination of these. They may be triggered by earthquakes, volcanic eruptions, soil saturation following rainfall or seepage or human activity such as removing vegetation, or construction of roads, railways or buildings on steep terrain. Gravity forces landslides to move. Most landslides are associated with periods of heavy rain or snow.

Landslides cause thousands of deaths and injuries and have huge financial costs each year.

Mudslides involve the rain-soaked earth on slopes and gullies suddenly rushing downhill, threatening people and buildings in its path. Usually they occur after heavy rain and without warning. Areas denuded by bushfires or clearing of vegetation are particularly susceptible to mudslides.

Prim-Ed Publishing   www.prim-ed.com

NATURAL DISASTERS 43

Avalanches, landslides and mudslides – 2

Use the text on page 43 to answer the questions.

1. Complete the sentences.

    (a) Avalanches are sometimes called _____

    (b) Avalanches may be caused by _____
    _____

    (c) Ninety-five per cent of people who are caught in an avalanche are trapped by a slide
    _____

    (d) The three main parts of an avalanche are _____
    _____

    (e) Three types of avalanches are _____
    _____   _____

    (f) The most dangerous avalanches are _____

    (g) Over _____ avalanches occur each year around

      the world in areas such as _____

      with the loss of more than _____ lives with _____

      more partly buried or injured.

2. Use the boxes below to explain how landslides and mudslides occur. You may use a diagram with labels if you wish, but you must use your own words.

Fact file
Ski patrols sometimes use large guns to shoot at freshly fallen snow on mountains. This triggers small avalanches and reduces the risk of large ones.

Alaskan avalanche poem

Avalanches, landslides, mudslides

1. Read the information about an avalanche disaster.

   On 12 April 1981, a chunk of ice the size of a school broke free from a glacier on Mount Sanford in Alaska and crashed into a snow-covered slope. It sent an avalanche of one million tonnes of snow downhill for a distance of 13 kilometres. A cloud of snow dust was visible 160 kilometres away. Miraculously, no-one was hurt by this extremely rare occurrence of such a huge avalanche.

2. Write your own poem about how it would feel, look, smell and sound to be in the path of such an avalanche. You can tell what happened and how you survived or avoided the avalanche. Use the plan below to assist you.

Type of poem		
Main events/action	**Sound words**	**Words about smell**
	Words about appearance	**Feeling words**
Other interesting words or rhyming words		

3. Write your draft on a separate sheet of paper then publish it with an appropriate illustration or artwork.

Fact file

On 30 October 1998, the side of Casita volcano collapsed during Hurricane Mitch, causing a landslide/mudflow which wiped out two towns in Nicaragua and killed more than 2000 people.

Prim-Ed Publishing   www.prim-ed.com

NATURAL DISASTERS

45

Avalanches, landslides, mudslides
Thredbo Ski Resort landslide

Objectives
- Reads information and answers questions about the Thredbo Ski Resort landslide.
- Researches and draws diagrams of equipment used to find survivors of the Thredbo Ski Resort disaster.

Worksheet information
- Pupils may work in pairs or small groups to complete the activity on page 49 as resources may be scarce. They should only complete those sections for which resources are readily available.
- Pupils may give an oral presentation about one of the 'gadgets'.
- Quiz questions relating to this section may be found on page xxiii.

Answers

page 48

1. Teacher check. Answers may include heavy snowfalls on the upper levels of the mountain or human intervention such as the construction of buildings or roads on a steep mountain.
2. Teacher check. Answers may include the need to see the views or construction to take into account the steep slope on the site or for tourist accommodation.
3. Once the local emergency services had viewed the site, they realised that the disaster was too large for them to cope with on their own.
4. (a) T (b) F (c) F (d) T (e) F (f) T (g) T (h) F (i) T

page 49

Teacher check

Cross-curricular activities
- Pupils write a newspaper article reporting the disaster.
- Residents of the other lodges said that the landslide sounded like a fighter jet. Ask the pupils to create a 'drama' using only bodily movement and sound effects to depict the movement of the landslide down the mountain into the buildings.
- Pupils write a diary entry as a resident of one of the other lodges, which describes the event.

Curriculum links

Page xxvii lists the main literacy and geography curriculum objectives covered by these activities. The final activity in this unit will help to teach the following curriculum objectives.

England	English	KS 2	• Use ICT-based reference materials and write in a range of forms.
Northern Ireland	Language and literacy	KS 2	• Read electronic texts on the Internet and write in different formats.
Republic of Ireland	English	5th/6th Class	• Find information through the use of IT and write in a variety of genres.
Scotland	English	Level C/D	• Use a search engine and write in different functional forms.
Wales	English	KS 2	• Use ICT-based reference materials and write in non-fiction forms; e.g explanations.

Thredbo Ski Resort landslide – 1

Avalanches, landslides, mudslides

The disaster

At approximately 11.35 pm on Wednesday 30 July 1997, most of the people at the Thredbo Ski Resort near Canberra, Australia, were sleeping soundly when 2000 cubic metres of earth, rock and trees from the side of the mountain plummeted down the 70° slope.

As it swept down the mountain, the landslide forced the four-storey Carinya Lodge 100 metres into an elevated car park and onto the Bimbadeen staff quarters below. Residents in the surrounding lodges were awakened by a sound like a fighter jet. The multi-level buildings were completely crushed. Debris and cars were strewn over the lower section of the mountain.

The rescue

Within minutes, the local emergency teams consisting of three fire/rescue units arrived on the scene. The Major Incident Coordination Centre in Sydney was notified immediately and expert rescue staff with specialist equipment responded to the disaster. The area was evacuated because of fears of broken gas lines and the threat of more landslides. Volunteers and emergency personnel were in place by 2.30 am. No sign of life was found in the first twenty-four hours. Rescuers used chainsaws, human chains, emergency lighting and eventually heavy equipment to clear the site searching for survivors. Work was made difficult by the darkness, freezing temperatures, the steepness of the hill and the unstable nature of the site.

By midnight the following day, only one body had been found. Huge concrete slabs (part of the car park), where rescuers felt many people could be trapped, hindered progress. Another two bodies were found by nightfall the following day.

At around 5.30 am on Saturday morning, fifty-five hours after the disaster had struck, movement was heard beneath huge concrete slabs. Fibre optic cameras were used to get a better idea of the survivor's position. A small pipe was passed through a gap to send warm air to raise the survivor's body temperature. Another tube enabled him to sip fluids to rehydrate his body. After ten hours of careful tunnelling and removal of rubble, a stretcher board was lowered into the hole to carry out the injured man. A team of 30 workers formed a chain to pass him along to a waiting ambulance. Stuart Diver, a 21-year-old ski instructor, was the only survivor of the Thredbo tragedy. A total of eighteen bodies were recovered in the aftermath of Australia's worst landslide disaster.

The result

The capacity of community services to carry out search and rescue operations was expanded as a result of this disaster. Different teams of rescuers learnt to cooperate more effectively and legislation was passed to assist in preventing a disaster of this type from happening again. This included restricting the building of properties on steeply sloping mountainous areas.

The survival of Stuart Diver is a remarkable example of a person in peak physical condition with an amazing will to survive.

Avalanches, landslides, mudslides

Thredbo Ski Resort landslide – 2

Use the text on page 47 to answer the questions.

1. What do you think caused the landslide which destroyed the two lodges at the Thredbo Ski Resort?

   _____

   _____

2. Why do builders in mountainous areas construct buildings which have more than one storey?

   _____

   _____

3. Why did the local emergency rescue teams notify another organisation once they had viewed the site of the landslide?

   _____

   _____

4. State *true* or *false*.

   (a) The area was at first evacuated because of the danger to rescuers from broken gas lines and further landslides.   True / False

   (b) A survivor was found within the first twenty-four hours.   True / False

   (c) It was difficult to carry out the rescue because another landslide caused more damage.   True / False

   (d) Rescuers thought that some survivors might be found under slabs of concrete which had formed part of the car park.   True / False

   (e) Movement from a survivor was found forty-eight hours after the landslide struck.   True / False

   (f) A small pipe and a tube of water kept the survivor alive until he could be rescued.   True / False

   (g) The survivor was carried out on a stretcher board along a human chain.   True / False

   (h) After the disaster, each emergency agency was given the ability to complete a rescue of this nature by itself.   True / False

   (i) This was Australia's worst landslide disaster.   True / False

---

Fact file

Rescuers had to use mobile phones and 'face-to-face' talking to communicate during the Thredbo disaster because no mutual communication channel existed between the various emergency agencies.

Grim gadgets

Avalanches, landslides, mudslides

During the Thredbo Ski Resort disaster, rescuers used a variety of devices to assist them to find and rescue survivors.

1. Working with a partner, use the library or Internet to find diagrams to illustrate these 'gadgets'. Draw and label them in the spaces provided.

KATO™ digger	helium-filled light

chainsaw	thermal imaging camera

seismic listening device	

2. On a separate sheet of paper, write a brief explanation of how each device works and what it is usually used for.

Fact file

Stuart Diver spent three nights in temperatures as low as –12 °C, developed hypothermia from wearing wet clothes for 65 hours and almost drowned after water entered his air space. His wife and friends all died.

Drought

Objectives

- Reads information and answers questions about drought.
- Plans a concert and creates an advertisement to raise awareness and funds for drought-affected farmers.

Worksheet information

- For the activity on page 53, Concert Creation!, pupils can work individually or in small groups. Pupils will need to consider their target audience and how they will raise the most money for their cause.
- In small groups, pupils create a television or radio commercial, an advertisement in a magazine or on a website or a billboard poster to advertise their concert. Pupils may need time out of sight of other groups to prepare and possibly rehearse their advertisement.
- Quiz questions relating to this section may be found on page xxiv.
- Emergency procedures relating to this section may be found on page xiv.

Answers

page 52

1. loss of stock (cattle and sheep)
   dust storms, loss of feed (grass etc.)
   unemployment
   bushfires, famine
   environmental damage such as soil erosion and vegetation loss
2. reservoirs, dams and rain tanks become dry
   little water for stock to drink and less growth of feed for them (grasses etc.)
   animals overgraze until all feed is gone
3. People not experiencing drought firsthand may become affected by it when prices of wheat and meat products rise.
4. It is determined if a town or area is experiencing drought by measuring rainfall in that area.
5. Fires are more likely to occur and spread during a drought due to the high temperatures and hot, dry winds.
6. Teacher check
7. Pop and rock stars raised awareness of the suffering occurring in Africa by performing in nine concerts around the world, called the Live 8 concerts.

page 53

Teacher check

Cross-curricular activities

- If possible, ask a farmer or a person who works in agriculture to come to the class and speak to the pupils about the impact drought has on crops and stock. Ensure the pupils understand that on large farms, irrigation is not a feasible option. Organise a class excursion to visit a farm.
- Make and use a rain gauge to record the amount of rainfall over one month. Use the Internet to find out the average rainfall for the town for each month. Pupils write a report that details whether the month that their data was recorded was below average, normal or above average. The report will include a graph representing the data they collected. Pupils research which months normally have the greatest or least amount of rainfall.
- Pupils work in small groups to research the Live 8 concerts. If available, they can view performances of the concert on the Internet. Pupils mark on a map where the concerts were held and note who performed at each. What were the concerts trying to achieve?

Curriculum links

Page xxvii lists the main literacy and geography curriculum objectives covered by these activities. The final activity in this unit will help to teach the following curriculum objectives.

England	English	KS 2	Write in a range of forms for a range of purposes and readers.
Northern Ireland	Language and literacy	KS 2	Write in different formats for a variety of purposes.
Republic of Ireland	English	5th/6th Class	Write in a variety of genres with a particular purpose and audience in mind.
Scotland	English	Level C	Write non-narrative texts for a given purpose and audience.
Wales	English	KS 2	Write for varied purposes.

Drought – 1

Drought is the lack of rainfall over a long period—perhaps a few months or even as long as a decade. Drought affects more people than any other natural disaster!

High temperatures and little rainfall affect crop growing and can have a devastating impact on communities, even causing widespread starvation.

Some effects of drought include:
- *loss of stock (cattle and sheep)*
- *dust storms*
- *loss of stock feed (grass etc.)*
- *unemployment*
- *bushfires*
- *famine*
- *environmental damage such as soil erosion and vegetation loss*

Farmers feel the effects of drought first and the most severely. Eventually, everyone else feels the impact. The lack of rain means reservoirs, farm dams and rain tanks become dry. There is little water for people or stock (cattle and sheep) to drink and there is less growth of crops and grass. The animals eat all of the available feed (called overgrazing), which results in the stock perishing from hunger or being culled by farmers before this occurs.

When there are shortages of crops, such as wheat, and meat, such as beef and lamb, the prices of these goods rise—so even people who are not experiencing the drought firsthand, will be affected by it.

The hot, dry winds of dust storms, common to droughts, blow away the topsoil, damaging crops. Also, when higher than normal temperatures occur, vegetation becomes stressed and may wither and die. In rural areas, drought can create unemployment. In some countries, such as Australia, when farmers have experienced a severe drought, the government offers them 'drought assistance'. This is money that will allow them to sustain their farms.

Disastrous forest and bushfires occur more frequently during a drought and can spread quickly as a result of the windy, dry conditions. Lives, sadly, are often lost.

Rainfall data is used to measure the severity of a drought. During a drought, governments may place restrictions on the public regarding their use of water to conserve what remains in the reservoirs; for example, odd or even house numbering determines which days people in Chicago, USA, and Perth, Australia, are allowed to water their lawns.

Droughts continue to cause much suffering, starvation and death in Africa, especially in areas such as Ethiopia and Sahel. Very few crops survive, and the little water that is available is often not clean drinking water, so people become ill.

Nine concerts were held simultaneously in July 2005, in London, Rome, Berlin, Paris, Philadelphia, Moscow, Tokyo, Ontario and Johannesburg to raise awareness of the starving and ill people of Africa. Performers such as Madonna, Robbie Williams, U2, Will Smith and the Black-eyed Peas performed for free at the Live 8 concerts.

Drought – 2

Use the text on page 51 to answer the questions.

1. List seven effects of drought.

   - _____
   - _____
   - _____
   - _____
   - _____
   - _____
   - _____

2. Use the chart below to show how a drought can result in the death of stock animals.

   [_____]
   ▼
   [_____]
   ▼
   [_____]
   ▼
   Animals perish from hunger or are culled by farmers before this occurs.

3. Describe how people not experiencing a drought firsthand may become affected by it.

   _____
   _____
   _____

4. How is it determined if a town or area is experiencing drought?

   _____
   _____
   _____

5. Why are fires more likely to occur and spread during a drought?

   _____
   _____

6. Do you think it is fair that people should be told when they can water their lawns so water for the community is conserved?

   Yes ◯ No ◯

   Explain your answer.

   _____
   _____
   _____

7. How are pop and rock stars helping to inform people about the suffering occurring in Africa?

   _____
   _____
   _____
   _____

Fact file

People living in Australia learn to live with drought as Australia is the driest inhabited continent.

Concert creation — Drought

Bob Geldof, a singer and humanitarian, has organised two successful concerts to raise awareness of the suffering of the people in Africa—Live Aid in 1985 and Live 8 in 2005. Nine concerts were held simultaneously in major cities across the world and pop and rock stars such as Robbie Williams, U2, Will Smith and the Black-eyed Peas performed for free.

Imagine that a terrible drought has occurred in your area, causing thousands of cattle and sheep to die, millions of hectares of crops to perish and people to suffer. You have been asked to organise a major concert that will raise money for the farmers and their families.

1. With your group, complete the plan to begin preparations for the concert.

Title of concert	Concert venue
Acts to perform at concert and predicted time limit of each act.	**Main target audience (age groups)**
	Cost of tickets
	Host of concert
	Emergency services attending
	Media covering concert
Other ways the message of 'drought relief for farmers' can be advertised during the concert (T-shirts etc.)	**Other (food to sell etc.)**

2. Now you must advertise your concert effectively so the maximum number of people will attend and the greatest amount of money will be raised. Choose one way to advertise your concert. In your group, create (and rehearse, if necessary) your advertisement and prepare to share it with the class.

- television commercial
- radio commercial
- magazine advertisement
- billboard poster
- website advert
- other ____

Fact file

The rings in the trunk of a tree reveal the history of drought in that area—in wet years the rings are thick, while in dry years, they are thin.

Storms and floods

Objectives

- Reads information and answers questions about storms and floods.
- Plans and writes a narrative.

Worksheet information

- Discuss areas in the local community that are prone to flooding (if any). What informs us of these areas—warning signs, measuring sticks etc.? What characteristics make these areas prone to flooding (low-lying area, rivers etc.)?
- Discuss any experiences the pupils may have had with severe storms or flooding. What safety measures did they take?
- Quiz questions relating to this section may be found on page xxiv.
- Emergency procedures relating to this section may be found on page xv.

Answers

page 56

1. (a) down loose objects
   (b) golf balls
   (c) electrocution, burns and hearing damage
   (d) a dam burst sending a wall of water to the town
2. lightning, hail stones, flash flooding, tornadoes
3. The severity of a storm can be measured by the number of insurance claims made to insurance companies.
4. Flash flooding – when a storm moves slowly and a great amount of rain falls upon a small area very quickly

   Prolonged rain – rain pouring for weeks at a time

5. Answers may include
   - destructive to environment
   - water can become contaminated causing people to become ill
   - debris caught under bridges, creating a dam and river to burst
   - crops, shops and houses ruined
   - carpets ruined, cars floating etc.
6. Teacher check

page 57

Teacher check

Cross-curricular activities

- In groups, pupils brainstorm words to describe a storm; for example, 'roaring', 'dark', 'light show', 'electrifying', 'static', 'anticipation', 'danger', 'thunder claps', 'rolling'.

  In pairs or individually, pupils write a poem about an approaching storm. Discuss the use of onomatopoeia—where the sound relates to the meaning, e.g. 'swish', 'plop', 'crunching'.

  Pupils choose from poetry styles such as:
  - **narrative poem:** tells or recites a story
  - **ballad:** narrative that contains rhyme with the last two lines of each stanza repeated
  - **sonnet:** fourteen lines, three stanzas of four lines with a rhyming couplet at the end
  - **ode:** same rhyming pattern (abcb), is the Greek word for song and celebrates or expresses admiration for something
- Use the Internet and library to discover why and how lightning occurs. Present findings as an information poster. Pupils may also present their findings verbally to small groups.
- What is El Ninõ? In small groups, pupils write an information report on this phenomenon. What effects does it have on the weather?

Curriculum links

Page xxvii lists the main literacy and geography curriculum objectives covered by these activities. The final activity in this unit will help to teach the following curriculum objectives.

England	English	KS 2	• Use a range of writing forms, including narratives.
Northern Ireland	Language and literacy	KS 2	• Use a variety of writing forms, including stories.
Republic of Ireland	English	5th/6th Class	• Write in a wide variety of genres, including narratives.
Scotland	English	Level C	• Develop imaginative writing and awareness of character, setting and action.
Wales	English	KS 2	• Use imaginative forms of writing, including stories.

Storms and floods – 1

Storms

Storms can have devastating effects on people and property. Storms generally affect small areas, compared to a cyclone or flood, but they can cause extreme damage to property and lives can be lost.

Severe storms can have wind gusts of 90 km/h or greater, hail with a diameter of 2 cm or more (with some as big as golf balls), flash flooding and sometimes even tornadoes. Thunderstorms can also produce lightning, which can kill. It is important during lightning strikes that the telephone is not used as phone systems can become charged, causing electrocution, burns and hearing damage.

A thunderstorm occurs when humid warm air near the ground is given an upward push (an updraft) by surface winds. The air rises quickly and cools. If it is joined by surrounding winds, a powerful thunderstorm can be created, with rain and hail (downdraft) hitting the ground.

When rain and hail drag air downwards in a rush, the strong gusts of wind can travel along the ground so fast that roofs are removed from houses and loose objects become deadly missiles.

Severe storms usually only last for about an hour and can be difficult to predict. How severe a storm is can be measured by the number of claims made to insurance companies. People try to recover money from insurance companies to buy new goods, replacing those that were damaged. Farmers claim money for their crops that may have been damaged by heavy rain or hailstones from the storm.

STAY SAFE during a STORM by:

staying inside

staying away from windows

tying down loose objects

disconnecting electrical appliances

staying off the telephone

hiding under a mattress or table

Floods

When a storm moves slowly, an excessive amount of rain can fall onto a small area very quickly, causing a flash flood. Drainage systems fail with so much water and overflow, and the soil is unable to absorb it. People can be caught trying to cross rivers with the water level rising rapidly around them.

Rain pouring for weeks at a time can also cause flooding. Rivers may swell and burst and dams break, wreaking havoc on towns and agriculture. In Morvi, India, in 1979, a dam burst sending a wall of water to the town. Five thousand lives were lost.

Floods are destructive of people, property and the environment. Water can become contaminated and germ-ridden from rubbish, sewage and poisonous chemicals and people may become ill.

Cattle, trees and other debris can become caught in a flood. If a large amount of debris becomes trapped under a bridge, a dam is created and rivers can burst! This water can ruin crops and destroy shops and houses.

About 10 cm of water will ruin your carpet, 15 cm of fast-flowing water will knock you off your feet and 60 cm of water will make your car float!

STAY SAFE during a FLOOD by:

having made an evacuation plan

keeping high and dry

wearing waterproof clothing and shoes

having fresh water available

securing any objects that may float

Storms and floods — 2

Storms and floods

Use the text on page 55 to answer the questions.

1. Complete the sentences.

    (a) Stay safe in a storm by tying …

    _____

    (b) A severe storm can have hailstones the size of …

    _____

    (c) People on the telephone during a lightning strike could experience …

    _____

    _____

    (d) Five thousand lives were lost in Morvi, India, when …

    _____

    _____

    _____

2. Strong, gusty wind is one way you know a storm is upon you. List four other signs of a severe storm or thunderstorm.

    _____

    _____

    _____

    _____

3. Explain how the severity of a storm is measured.

    _____

    _____

    _____

    _____

    _____

4. There are two ways flooding may occur. Describe each.

Flash flooding:	Prolonged rain:

5. List two effects flooding may have on towns and people.

    _____

    _____

6. Read the information about how a thunderstorm occurs and draw a diagram on the back of this sheet explaining it. Add labels and information to the diagram.

    Fact file

    Lightning can and often does strike the same place more than once. During a lightning storm at night, an object may glow blue, showing that it may be about to be struck, so run! This is called St Elmo's fire.

NATURAL DISASTERS

Prim-Ed Publishing   www.prim-ed.com

The storm spotter!

Storms and floods

On the outside, Charlie looks like a typical school gardener. He tends to the flowers, keeps the sports field in shape with his ride-on mower and retrieves lost balls from the library roof.

Unknown to the pupils at Richmond Primary, Charlie is also a storm spotter—always on the lookout for spectacular storms. Charlie is part of a network of volunteers who provide 'on-the-spot' information about powerful and damaging storms via laptop computers.

Charlie has left school in a hurry today, not realising that two stowaways are hiding in the back of his truck. He races towards the storm …

You and a friend are the stowaways in Charlie's truck. What happens when you reach the storm? Are you discovered? Do you become a storm spotter too?

1. Plan a narrative that continues the story of you and the storm spotter.

Characters: • Charlie • • •	Genre: • adventure ☐ • humorous ☐ • horror ☐ • supernatural ☐	Setting: (Describe it – what can you see, hear, smell, taste?)
Introduction:		
Middle: Event 1	**Middle:** Event 2	**Middle:** Event 3
End: (Resolve the problems and tie up loose ends)		

Electrical light show — Directly above us! — Deafening roar!

Fact file

Hailstones weighing up to 1 kilogram are reported to have killed 92 people in Bangladesh on 14 April 1986.

Tornadoes

Objectives

- Reads information and answers questions about tornadoes.
- Conducts and evaluates science experiments about making a 'tornado'.

Worksheet information

- Pupils need not understand exactly how tornadoes are formed except that different temperatures of air often at different wind speeds and levels collide, causing one lot of air to spiral quickly upwards.
- Quiz questions relating to this section may be found on page xxv.
- Emergency procedures relating to this section may be found on page xvi.

Answers

page 60

1. (a) storms (b) funnels (c) thunderstorm (d) hurricane (e) twisters (f) 12 200 (g) damage (h) 400 (i) path (j) 80.5 (k) 1.5 (l) cool (m) quickly (n) Tornado Alley

2.

		Speeds	Damage
Classification	F–0	65–115 km/h	causes chimney damage; tree branches broken
	F–1	116–180 km/h	mobile homes pushed off foundations or overturned
	F–2	181–250 km/h	considerable damage; mobile homes demolished; trees uprooted
	F–3	251–330 km/h	roofs and walls torn apart; trains overturned; cars thrown
	F–4	331–418 km/h	well-built walls levelled
	F–5	419–512 km/h	homes lifted off foundations and carried considerable distance; cars thrown as far as 100 metres

3. Houses appear to explode because the air pressure within the vortex is extremely low. Inside the building the air pressure is normal, so when the tornado passes over, the air inside the building expands, creating an explosion.

page 61

Teacher check

Cross-curricular activities

- Pupils design their own experiments to create a tornado.
- Pupils use an atlas and a map of USA to plot and colour the states which make up 'Tornado Alley.'
- Pupils write an eyewitness account of a tornado from the point of view of a 'tornado chaser'.

Curriculum links

Page xxvii lists the main literacy and geography curriculum objectives covered by these activities. The final activity in this unit will help to teach the following curriculum objectives.

England	Science	KS 2	• Use simple equipment and materials appropriately, make observations and draw conclusions.
Northern Ireland	Science	KS 2	• Record, analyse and present information.
Republic of Ireland	Science	5th/6th Class	• Observe, offer explanations and draw conclusions.
Scotland	Science	Level C	• Make appropriate observations and explain what happens in experiments, drawing on scientific knowledge.
Wales	Science	KS 2	• Use equipment and resources correctly, make observations and draw conclusions.

Tornadoes – 1

Tornadoes are violent storms characterised by violently twisting funnels of air, usually caused by a thunderstorm or hurricane. 'Twisters' can grow to over 12 200 metres high. Tornadoes can cause tremendous destruction as a result of wind speeds of 400 kilometres per hour or more. Wind-blown debris also adds to the damage. The path of destruction may be over 1.5 kilometres wide and 80.5 kilometres long. Heavy objects such as cars and cows can be sucked up and spun around like pieces of confetti. Even houses appear to explode!

Tornadoes are caused when cool air encounters a layer of warm air, forcing the warm air to rise quickly. The diagrams below show how a tornado is formed.

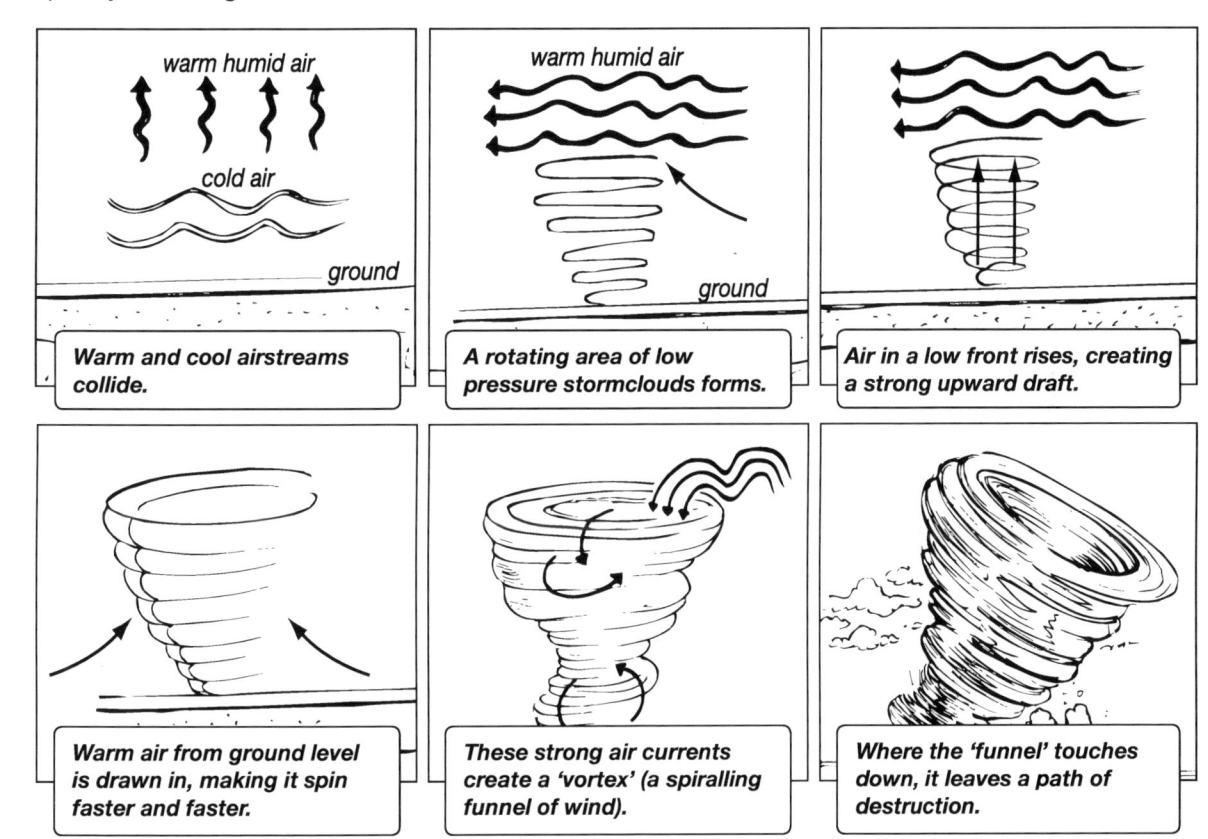

Warm and cool airstreams collide.	A rotating area of low pressure stormclouds forms.	Air in a low front rises, creating a strong upward draft.
Warm air from ground level is drawn in, making it spin faster and faster.	These strong air currents create a 'vortex' (a spiralling funnel of wind).	Where the 'funnel' touches down, it leaves a path of destruction.

Tornadoes are measured on the Fujita Pearson Scale and classified:

F–0: wind speeds of between 65 and 115 km/h; causes chimney damage; tree branches broken

F–1: wind speeds of between 116 and 180 km/h; mobile homes pushed off foundations or overturned

F–2: wind speeds of between 181 and 250 km/h; considerable damage; mobile homes demolished; trees uprooted

F–3: wind speeds of between 251 and 330 km/h; roofs and walls torn down; trains overturned; cars thrown

F–4: wind speeds of between 331 and 418 km/h; well-built walls levelled

F–5: wind speeds of between 419 and 512 km/h; homes lifted off foundations and carried considerable distances; cars thrown as far as 100 metres

'Tornado Alley' is an area in the USA which experiences the most intense killer tornadoes likely to occur—F–4 and F–5. Tornado Alley incorporates a large number of states: Texas, Louisiana, Arkansas, Oklahoma, Kansas, Nebraska, South Dakota, North Dakota, Iowa, Missouri, Illinois, Indiana, and some areas of Colorado, Minnesota, Ohio, Kentucky, Tennessee and Wyoming.

Tornadoes – 2

Complete the cloze using the text on page 59.

1. Tornadoes are violent _____(a) which have twisting _____(b) of air. They are usually caused by a _____(c) or _____(d). They are often called '_____'(e) and may grow to a height of over _____(f) metres. Tornadoes can cause a vast amount of _____(g) due to the fact that they can travel at speeds of _____(h) km/h or more. Tornadoes can result in a _____(i) of destruction over a distance of _____(j) kilometres and a width of _____(k) kilometres. Tornadoes are the result of _____(l) air forcing warm air to rise very _____.(m) One of the worst areas in the world to experience tornadoes is '_____'(n) in the USA.

2. Complete the table which shows the different classifications of tornadoes on the Fujita Pearson Scale.

Classification	Speeds	Damage
F–0		
F–1		
F–2		
F–3		
F–4		
F–5		

3. Explain, scientifically, how houses can appear to 'explode'.

_____
_____
_____
_____

Fact file

Waterspouts are weak tornadoes that form over water. Occasionally, they move inland to become tornadoes.

Tornado experiments — Tornadoes

1. Collect the relevant equipment and carry out the following experiments, both of which show how to create a tornado. Tick each step as you complete it.

Experiment A

Materials:
- two 2-litre plastic bottles (lids removed)
- strong tape, for example, duct tape
- food colouring

Procedure:
1. Fill one bottle about two-thirds full of water and add a few drops of food colouring. ☐
2. Use the tape to join the two bottles together securely at the mouth. ☐
3. Turn the bottles so that the one filled with water is at the top. ☐
4. Rotate the bottles in a circular motion. You should see the effect of a tornado where the top bottle meets the bottom one! ☐

Experiment B

Materials:
- 250 g jar with lid
- water
- vinegar
- clear dishwashing liquid
- glitter

Procedure:
1. Fill the jar three-quarters full of water. ☐
2. Add one teaspoon of vinegar and one teaspoon of dishwashing liquid. ☐
3. Sprinkle in a small amount of glitter. ☐
4. Close the lid and twist the jar to see a tornado-like vortex form. ☐

2. Evaluate the two experiments by answering the following questions.

   (a) Which experiment worked better? | **A** | **B** | Why? _____

   _____

   (b) What changes or improvisations did you have to make to the experiments to get them to work properly?

A	**B**

Fact file
People called 'tornado chasers' or 'storm chasers' closely follow tornadoes to witness the spectacle firsthand, to gather scientific data or to take photos; not a job for the fainthearted!

Bushfires

Objectives

- *Reads information and answers questions about bushfires.*
- *Completes word study activities relating to bushfires.*

Worksheet information

- Some of the terms used in the text on page 63 may need to be discussed and clarified for pupils; for example, ignition, asphyxiation, flammable, embers, dehydration and regeneration. Pupils should be encouraged to use contextual information to determine word meaning.
- Quiz questions relating to this section may be found on page xxv.
- Emergency procedures relating to this section may be found on page xvi.

Answers

page 64

1. (a) wildfire
   (b) They can cause loss of life, injury, stock and wildlife losses and damage to property and crops.
2. (a) flammable vegetation
   (b) They produce oil that burns fast and hot, often producing fireballs.
   (c) Answers may include: droughts, dry weather, high temperatures, strong winds.
3. (a) Lightning
   (b) So that they will not start a bushfire.
   (c) Teacher check
4. (a) Their farm machinery might start a fire that they will not be able to control.
   (b) Teacher check
5. Teacher check

page 65

1. (a) dehydration (b) grader   (c) flammable
   (d) ignition   (e) Foliage   (f) regenerate
   (g) asphyxiation (h) firebreak   (i) Ash
   (j) embers   (k) fuel   (l) Smoke
2. (a) Arsonists cost lives
   (b) Teacher check

Cross-curricular activities

- Research the causes and effects of lightning and prepare a poster warning people about the dangers of lightning.
- Dramatise incidents related to bushfires; for example, before, during or after a bushfire in particular settings—a house, a car, or the bush.

Curriculum links

Page xxvii lists the main literacy and geography curriculum objectives covered by these activities. The final activity in this unit will help to teach the following curriculum objectives.

England	English	KS 2	• Use vocabulary with more complex meanings.
Northern Ireland	Language and literacy	KS 2	• Acquire and develop a vocabulary.
Republic of Ireland	English	5th/6th Class	• Experience a growing elaboration and sophistication in the use of vocabulary.
Scotland	English	Level D	• Use specialist vocabulary from other curricular areas.
Wales	English	KS 2	• Extend and enrich vocabulary through activities that focus on words and their meanings.

Bushfires – 1

What are bushfires?

One of the most destructive forces in nature is a wildfire or, as it is called in Australia, a bushfire. It is a fire in the country that often features heavy smoke, strong wind and showers of embers. Bushfires become disasters when they cause loss of life, injury, stock and wildlife losses or damage to property and crops.

Causes of bushfires

A bushfire needs oxygen, fuel and an ignition source.

Fuel is provided by flammable vegetation. In Australia, the oil produced by eucalyptus trees burns hot and fast, often creating fireballs which engulf the upper storey of the forest. Droughts, dry weather, high temperatures and additional oxygen from strong winds all contribute to bushfires.

Ignition most commonly results from lightning strikes. Other fires are either deliberately or accidentally started by people. Out-of-control fires lit by farmers, campfires and fires caused by farming machinery in hot dry conditions, often start bushfires. People who deliberately light fires are called arsonists.

Effects of bushfires

The heat, smoke and ash from bushfires can affect people, animals, plants and property.

Injury and loss of life are caused by radiant heat, dehydration, asphyxiation and falling materials. Stock and native animals are at similar risk. Some animals, like wombats, can burrow beneath the ground until the danger has passed.

Crops are often totally destroyed by bushfires. Many trees, however, lose their foliage and have their bark burnt, but are able to regenerate. Some plant growth can even be improved following a bushfire.

Houses are often destroyed in bushfires because embers fall on close-by trees and bushes or catch in gutters and ignite leaves and other dry material trapped there. Often there isn't enough water or hoses to get the water to the fire.

Spot fires

Firefighting

People should prepare and protect their homes by removing flammable materials and having water and hoses available.

Bushfire fighting is the responsibility of some professional firefighters but local volunteer firefighters play a vital role. They use graders and bulldozers to clear firebreaks and often back-burn an area in front of the fire to remove flammable vegetation. Helicopters and other aircraft are used to drop water and to provide information about the direction and size of fires.

Weather forecasts about wind direction and rain can be of vital importance.

Bushfires – 2

Answer the questions using the text provided on page 63.

1. (a) What is another name for a bushfire?

   (b) Why are bushfires dangerous?

2. (a) What is the fuel of bushfires?

   (b) Why are eucalyptus trees so dangerous?

   (c) Name three factors that contribute to bushfires.

3. (a) What is the most common natural cause of bushfires?

   (b) Why is it very important to make sure campfires are extinguished?

   (c) Describe how you would extinguish a camp fire.

4. (a) Explain why farmers are often banned from harvesting crops on very hot and windy days.

   (b) If you lived in the country, how would you protect your home from bushfires?

5. Would you like to be a bushfire fighter? Yes ☐ No ☐ Give two reasons.

Fact file
South-eastern Australia is considered to be the area of greatest bushfire risk in the world.

Bushfire vocabulary

Bushfires

1. Find a word from the text on page 63 to complete each sentence.

    (a) Loss of water or other fluids is _____ .

    (b) A _____ is a vehicle with a blade at the front, used to level roads.

    (c) If something is _____ , it is easily set alight.

    (d) The process of starting a fire is called _____ .

    (e) _____ is the leaves of a plant.

    (f) To _____ something is to bring it into existence again.

    (g) Choking due to lack of oxygen is _____ .

    (h) A strip of land cleared to stop a fire from spreading is a _____ .

    (i) _____ is the powder left when something has been burnt.

    (j) Small live coals from a fire are _____ .

    (k) Anything that burns to give heat is referred to as _____ .

    (l) _____ is a cloud of gas and tiny particles given off when something burns.

2. (a) Cross out all of the letters in the word snake that you can see in the fire truck. The letters left over make a message. Write it in the box provided.

    (b) Do you agree with this message? Explain.

    _____

    _____

    _____

    Fact file
    Aboriginal Australians learnt over thousands of years that they could encourage plant growth by controlled burning.